MW00440349

THE SUNNI-SHIA CONFLICT

ALSO BY NATHAN GONZALEZ

Engaging Iran:

The Rise of a Middle East Powerhouse and America's Strategic Choice

THE SUNNI-SHIA CONFLICT

Understanding Sectarian Violence in the Middle East

NATHAN GONZALEZ

Gonzalez, Nathan, 1979—
   The Sunni-Shia conflict: understanding sectarian violence in the Middle East / Nathan Gonzalez. — 1st ed.

Includes bibliographical references and index.
ISBN 13: 978-0-9842252-0-0
ISBN 10: 0-9842252-0-X
Library of Congress Control Number: 2009935988

Printed in the Unuited States of America on acid-free paper.

Nortia Press
27525 Puerta Real 100-467
Mission Viejo, California 92691
U.S.A.

www.NortiaPress.com

Map by Jillian Luff, MAPgrafix

To the Men and Women of the U.S. Military

Map of Middle Eastern Regions

* Modern countries appear in gray

CONTENTS

Preface

Speeding down the streets of East Beirut in his SUV, a former militia leader points out signs of political and religious identity stenciled on the war-battered cement walls. "See those crosses?," asks "Michael," a former high-ranking officer with the Lebanese Forces. "They're ours." The LF was an umbrella Christian militia responsible for some of the most gruesome atrocities of the fifteen-year Lebanese Civil War (1975-1990). Today, it's a political party that is theoretically unarmed.

It is here, straddling the makeshift border that divides the eastern neighborhood of Ayn al-Rammanah from the Hezbollah-held suburbs of South Beirut, where I get a glimpse of the lasting impact that sectarian conflicts can have on a society long after cease-fires are signed and life supposedly returns to normal. Some outposts facing the dividing line are manned by Lebanese army units, while adjacent ones are LF political offices spilling over with veteran fighters of the civil war; aging men who are unemployed and carry the burden of stubborn memories from a brutal conflict. Here, they seek to defend the concept of Lebanon as a Christian nation, posting a network of lookouts throughout East Beirut, lest Hezbollah decide to come in, just as it had intruded into Sunni West Beirut in May 2008.

Yet without brandishing their weapons, this group of ex-militiamen looks more like a rag-tag neighborhood watch than the military force its supporters claim it to be. Asked whether these men could ever hold their own against Hezbollah, a seasoned and disciplined Shia organization that claimed military victory over Israel in the July 2006 War, Michael doesn't hesitate: "We'll fight to the last man." His statement, despite its empty bravado, is not hypothetical; not in his mind at least. "There will be a civil war in one, maybe two years," he says. "And we'll be ready."

Michael's outlook is in the minority among Lebanese Christians, and the country has come a long way toward achieving a level of sectarian coexistence. Yet it would be foolish to ignore that prior to the civil war, Lebanon had been considered a bastion of democracy and tolerance in the Middle East—Beirut was "the Paris of the Middle East." In Iraq, the United States is in the midst of withdrawing its troops, with many in the policy community remaining optimistic that the 2007 U.S. troop surge was such a success and it is now time to move on. But Iraq, like Lebanon, does not exist in a vacuum; its sectarian fissures will not be healed in a few years' time, not as long as outside interests have competing stakes in its future. After all, it is only when outside interests are brought to bear on local conflicts that we witness some of the worst episodes of sectarian violence in the Middle East. If the United States and the international community do not deal with geopolitical disputes, they will never be able to heal the scars of sectarian conflict in Iraq, Lebanon, and beyond.

In many ways, this book is a response to some commonly held assumptions about the nature of sectarian war. The oft-told adage that "they have always hated each other" can be an attractive one, particularly when it leads policymakers in the United States and across the world to believe that there is nothing they can do to help ameliorate the civil strife in Middle Eastern countries. But resignation is no longer an option when observers begin to understand that sectarian conflict is not one of local-level, individually internalized religious obsession, but rather it is a consequence of regional forces pulling and tugging, seeking to use weak, ungovernable countries as battlegrounds for proxy conflicts they dare not launch on a level of total war. While we will not likely see a clash between the armies of Egypt, Saudi Arabia and Jordan and those of Iran any time soon, this does not mean that a conflict between these nations hasn't started yet, with Iraq acting as a the principal battleground. The sooner the international community understands this, the more innocent lives will be spared.

The following chapters will explore various sources of conflict and war and how they are playing out in the Middle East today. Chapter 1 begins with an introduction to the concept of the "three cataysts" of sectarian conflict, forces that lay behind some of the most violent episodes of sectarian violence in the region. Chapters 2-5 provide a historical narrative of how the Sunni and Shia branches developed into parallel and often competing orthodoxies, always with the help of powerful empires that had an interest in using religion as a political tool to divide and conquer.

Chapter 6 brings us to the modern era. The chapter focuses on the recent history of Iraq, including its faulty foundations borne out of Ottoman and British colonialism. Chapter 7 discusses the large-scale sectarian violence of the Lebanese civil war, which in many ways was a precursor to Iraq's post-2003 experience. The comparable sectarian nature of Iraq and Lebanon makes the Lebanese civil war and its aftermath a lasting example of how sectarian tensions can remain even after cease-fires have been brokered and calm appears to be taking hold.

Chapter 8 recounts the U.S. invasion and its immediate aftermath, and introduces the major players of the Iraqi civil conflict. Lastly, chapter 9 provides some policy suggestions for achieving long-term, sustainable stability in Iraq, a monumental but indispensable task for the United States—a country that is wholly responsible for the current state of affairs in Iraq.

In a book of limited length, it is important to note what it does not seek to do. For one, this book does not offer a general theory of how sectarian conflicts emerge around the world. Rather, it is an explanation of the trends that have generated the bulk of sectarian violence in the Middle East specifically.

Because the book focuses on sectarian rather than ethnic violence, it will not deal at great length with Kurdish and other separatist movements, which certainly have a profound impact on the political landscape of the region. Also, the Sunni-Shia divisions outside of the Middle East, particularly in Pakistan, will not be explored.

Finally, this book does not deal with the peaceful relations between the vast majority of Sunnis and Shias in the world, which represent the norm rather than the exception. Because this is a study of conflict and not human kindness, Islam's greatest legacy of knowledge, peace, and tolerance will inevitably be obscured.

This project would not have been possible without the generous help of numerous people, a few of whom space permits me to mention. My friends Mahsa Maleki and Michael Clovis were extremely helpful in combing through early drafts of the book. Dr. Houri Berberian at California State University-Long Beach generously took the time to provide suggestions on a later draft, while Howard Vicini and my colleague Thea Sircair at UCLA gave their insights on how to make parts of the text more readable. A special thanks is owed to Dr. Lina Kreidie at the University of California-Irvine, who was kind enough to show me around parts of her native Beirut. In addition, a couple of anonymous reviewers made excellent suggestions regarding the content and overall structure of the manuscript. Any shortcomings found in this book are entirely my own, though these would have been far more numerous had it not been for the time these and many other dear friends were kind enough to provide.

Nathan Gonzalez
August 20, 2009
Los Angeles, CA.

Author's Note

The following is an overview and analysis of sectarian conflict tailored to the general public. Since the current sectarian divisions are rooted in the past, I introduce concepts and personalities from Middle Eastern history that may be unfamiliar to many readers. To make things easier, I have posted a glossary of terms, names and places on my website.

Because topics that deal with Islam and the Middle East tend to invite controversy, it always helps to be aware of an author's philosophical perspective. This is why I have included a companion essay at the back of this book, which lays out my analytical point of view as clearly as possible.

As for spelling Arabic and Persian words in our alphabet, I've focused on a balance between simplicity and accurate pronunciation. I've left words such as Mecca, Medina, and other commonly used proper nouns in the typical American spelling, and whenever possible I have avoided using diacritical marks for *'ayn* (') and *hamzah* ('). Names of Iranian places and people have been spelled to approximate the Persian pronunciation, while Islamic terms have largely been spelled to mimic the Arabic.

For the complete glossary, along with book discussion topics, visit www.NathanGonzalez.com.

Prologue

WHAT IS ISLAM?

More often than not, studying a particular faith involves taking a snap-shot in time. To answer simple questions about the tenets of a religion, it is often necessary to look at how that faith is practiced today, at this very moment. Such a glimpse will help us answer broad questions using state-ments like, "Christians believe that Jesus is the Son of God," or "Jews don't proselytize," or "Muslims fast during the holy month of Ramadan." While basically correct today, these generalized statements were not al-ways true.

Religion, like language, political ideology, and national identity, is an ever-changing phenomenon and not a rigid collection of laws. To re-ally understand religion, we have to take space and time into account. That said, it is usually helpful to review the kinds of common definitions one would find in the dictionary, particularly when it comes to compli-cated terms such as "Sunni" and "Shia," or "Islam" for that matter. In this prologue, I lay out the basics of the Muslim faith, a snapshot of a religion practiced by nearly 2 billion people around the world today.

A monotheistic faith, Islam (meaning Submission) embraces the concept of a single god—the God of Abraham and Jacob—as the sole cre-ator and source of salvation. Recognizing the prophets of other world re-ligions, particularly Judaism, as true communicators of God's will, Muslims place Muhammad as the last one: the Seal of the Prophets. Muslims revere Jesus of Nazareth as a true prophet, though they do not view him as the Son of God.

Officially, Muhammad is not granted any supernatural attributes, though he is generally considered to be an ideal, even infallible man. Conscious of the ban against idolatry, conservative Muslims have usually abstained from depicting the face of the Prophet in artwork. As a result Islamic art has departed from the Christian tradition of painting Jesus and saints in fresco and instead has focused on calligraphy and decorative masonry as aesthetic expressions of Muslim culture.

The basic practices of the Muslim faith are embodied in the five pillars of Islam, which form the foundation of law and jurisprudence. The five pillars are as follows:

1. **Bearing witness (*Shahadah*)**: This pertains to "witnessing," or declaring acceptance of the faith: "I bear witness that there is no god but God, and I bear witness that Muhammad is the Prophet of God." (Arabic: "*Ashhadu 'al-la ilahu ila Allah, wa ashhadu anna Muhammadun Rasoul Allah.*") Today, this proclamation is all that is needed to convert to Islam, though the Shia may add a third clause to the sentence: "and Ali is a servant of God." (Arabic: "*wa 'Aliun Waliyu Allah.*")

2. **Prayer (*Salat*)**: Muslims are required to pray five times a day, facing the Ka'ba, a cubic sanctuary in the Grand Mosque of Mecca. Mecca, the holiest city of Islam, and Medina, the second, are in the Hijaz region of Saudi Arabia.

3. **Alms-giving (*Zakat*)**: Muslims are required to donate a portion of their earnings and assets to help the poor. This is not an institutional tax, as that levied by European churches. Rather, it can be given in any number of ways, especially through private charities. Shias are asked to give an additional contribution, called *khums* (literally, "one-fifth"), comprising 20 percent of the believer's net income, which helps maintain holy sites and other religious institu-

tions.

4. Fasting during Ramadan (*Sawm*): For the entire lunar month of Ramadan, Muslims who are healthy enough to do so fast from dawn until dusk. Like Yom Kippur in Judaism, Ramadan acts as a channel to cleanse one's sins and offers a window of empathy toward the less fortunate. Feeding the hungry also becomes an important function of believers during this month.

5. Pilgrimage (*Hajj*): Every able-bodied Muslim who can afford the trip is required to take the pilgrimage to Mecca at least once in a lifetime, as Muhammad did in 632.

With the exception of Israel, all Middle Eastern countries have a Muslim majority. The Middle East generally encompasses the region between Iran in the east, the Arabian Peninsula in the south, and the countries of North Africa in the far west. But what many scholars call the "Greater Middle East" reaches well into the domains of the former Iranian, or Persian Empire, including Central Asian countries such as Afghanistan, Uzbekistan, Turkmenistan, and Tajikistan, and parts of South Asia such as Pakistan and Bangladesh.

The vast majority of Muslim countries are dominated by the Sunni sect, though most have considerable pockets of Shia faithful. The predominantly Shia countries in the region are Iran (87 percent Shia), Bahrain (65–70 percent), Iraq (60–65 percent), and Lebanon (a 40 percent plurality). The former Soviet Republic of Azerbaijan, which is slightly outside the region, in the Caucasus, is around 67 percent Shia.

Sunni Islam

The name "Sunni," loosely translated as "traditional," or "orthodox," refers to the political camp that accepted the succession of leadership in the Muslim state after the death of the Prophet Muhammad in AD 632. Because the vast majority of Muslims (90 percent) subscribe to the Sunni branch, it is often referred to simply as Islam, with no unique clarification needed. It should be noted from the outset, however, that neither

Sunnis nor Shias are monolithic groups in and of themselves, as each branch contains several, often competing theological schools of thought.

The Sunni-Shia split, at its core, originated with the appointment of Abu Bakr, a close companion of the Prophet, to be leader of the emerging Muslim Empire in 632. Plainly speaking, Sunnis are the people who accepted Abu Bakr as their political and religious leader. As with any religious history, there are divergent accounts about the events that led to his appointment. One viewpoint is laid out by esteemed Muhammad biographer W. Montgomery Watt, who wrote that the Prophet

> had made no arrangements for the continued administration of the affairs of the Islamic state except that he had appointed Abu-Bakr to lead the prayers. The end had come fairly suddenly, and for a time there was confusion in Medina, until it was agreed that Abu-Bakr should be his caliph, or successor. The funeral took place on the night between Tuesday and Wednesday, not in the usual burial-ground but within [the Prophet's wife] 'A'ishah's apartment.[1]

The choice of Abu Bakr rankled the partisans of Ali, the Prophet's cousin, son-in-law, and de facto baby brother (Ali's father, Abu Talib, had taken the orphaned Muhammad into his household at the age of eight). Though Ali did not battle Abu Bakr, he never let go of his claims to leadership. Ali eventually took executive power over the Muslim Empire as the fourth caliph but the battles only escalated, and during his reign the powerful faction that eventually gave rise to the Sunnis waged a civil war against him.

Officially speaking, the Sunnis tend to view the leadership of caliphs (those who succeeded the Prophet) as human and prone to fallibility. Apart from considering Ali as the last of the four "Rightly Guided Caliphs," Sunnis do not grant him any level of divine inspiration or religious purity beyond that of the others. The tendency in Sunni Islam is to focus less on the leadership of individuals and more on the literal expressions of religion.

The four dominant schools of theology in Sunni Islam are Hanafi, Maliki, Shafi, and Hanbali, each receiving its name from an eponymous founder. In general, the Hanafi school, which is practiced largely in Turkey, parts of Afghanistan, and the Indian subcontinent, tends to be more liberal, while Hanbali, embraced largely in the Arabian Peninsula, is the most conservative.

Perhaps the most infamous figure associated with Hanbali thought is Osama bin Laden, a follower of the writings of Ibn Taymiyya, a thirteenth-century Hanbali scholar who was a fundamentalist even by the standards of his contemporaries. Ibn Taymiyya wrote during a time when Mongols held control over much of the Middle East and European Crusaders lay at the region's doorstep, and he advocated the use of holy struggle, or *jihad*, against the nonbelieving occupiers. This belief in the need to cleanse the lands against occupiers (real and perceived) is the backbone of the modern jihadist movement, one that in recent decades has been gaining traction in the Middle East and around the world.

Also loosely associated with Hanbali thought are the Salafis, individuals who yearn to live as much as possible like the Companions of the Prophet did in the seventh century. Salafis tend to reject the division of Sunni Islam into four schools, preferring instead to focus on developing the expertise to verify the authenticity of various *Hadith*, the oral traditions of the Prophet, and thus abandon many of the later juridical arguments that arose with the four schools. Within the Salafi movement one finds the so-called Wahhabis of Saudi Arabia, who are given this derogatory brand after Muhammad ibn Abd al-Wahhab—a fundamentalist fighter who allied with the rising Saudi family in the eighteenth century to consolidate power over the Arabian Peninsula, eventually giving rise to the Kingdom of Saudi Arabia.

Many ultraconservative Sunnis share a passionate hatred for Shiism and place significant emphasis on a strict reading of monotheism. Saudi religious authorities have even tried to "concrete over the existing foundations" of the site of the Prophet Muhammad's birth, lest it fall prey to idolatry.[2] This charge of idolatry is one of the most serious leveled against the Shia, who venerate key figures from the family, or House, of the Prophet Muhammad, including Ali himself.

Shia Islam

The Shia are the Party of Ali, or *Shi'at 'Ali*. They believe that the selection of Abu Bakr as successor to Muhammad was a usurpation—a *coup d'état*. The Shia contend that the correct line of succession after the Prophet's death should have been familial, stemming from Ali and his wife Fatima (who was the Prophet's daughter). The Shia consider Ali to be their first Imam, and while the word *imam* literally means leader, in the case of Shiism it refers to a particular office that transcends human fallibility. The Twelver Shia community, which is predominant in Iran, Iraq, and Lebanon, recognizes the existence of twelve such Imams, the last of whom went into a period of extended or "Great" Occultation in 941. Since then, believers have awaited his return as the *Mahdi*, or Messiah.

The most important moment in the collective memory of the Shia is the Battle of Karbala of 680, which was fought on Iraqi soil. In that battle Imam Husayn, son of Ali and grandson of the Prophet, was martyred at the hand of the caliph Yazid, a Sunni who ordered the Imam's head, and eventually got it. Every year Shia communities around the world meet in small and large congregations, often spilling out into the streets, to commemorate their fallen leader Husayn. "Ya, Husayn!" they cry out, beating their chests in pounding unison. Through this, they hope to somehow share in the pain of their Imam and imagine fighting and suffering his fate alongside him.

Structurally speaking, Shiism maintains a hierarchy that is simply not found in Sunni Islam. Shia clerics, unlike their Sunni counterparts, have kept alive a version of the charismatic authority once held by the Imams, and unlike Sunni clerics, they have significant latitude in interpreting Islamic law. In the present day when high-ranking Shia clerics cannot find the answer to a question through the Qur'an, the oral traditions of the Prophet and the Imams, and other sources of law, they can make what amounts to a legislative decision, though it is not referred to in those terms. This explains why the Islamic Republic of Iran has violently persecuted gays, while at the same time it legally allows for sex changes, a modern medical procedure that clearly had not been discussed in the holy texts of centuries past. This latitude to interpret new religious questions stems from a concept called *ijtihad* (more on this in chapter 4).

In modern times, Shia believers have chosen which clerics to follow from among several highly qualified scholars. These clerics, called *marjatu al-taqlid*, or Source of Emulation, are free to give their interpretation of Islamic law and practice ijtihad. Believers associate themselves with a given *marja* and follow his advice on all issues of life, from whether artificial insemination is permissible under Islam, to whether an Imam can be portrayed in a movie. Grand Ayatollah Ali al-Sistani of Iraq is one such marja, and his tacit acceptance of America's military presence in Iraq in 2003 considerably limited Shia antagonism to the foreign presence in the country. (As difficult as security was for U.S. troops, things could have been much worse had the entire Shia community engaged in a general uprising.)

Shia hierarchy has no strict organizational chart. A cleric's rank is often a telltale sign of his following and the collegial respect he inspires, so essentially the clerical cream rises to the top. That said, there are some basic definitions of authority. A *mullah* may be a local prayer leader or teacher, while a *hujjatu al-Islam* (Proof of Islam) attains his title only after finishing courses in philosophy, jurisprudence, and rhetoric at the seminary. The next step is *ayatollah* (Sign of God), and after that *ayatollah al-uzma* (Grand Ayatollah), who is also a marjatu al-taqlid.

After the Iranian Revolution of 1978–79 and the subsequent rise of Grand Ayatollah Ruhollah Khomeini to power in Iran, the balance of power has shifted to a small number of Shia clergy in ways that were previously unimaginable. While in modern times clerics had played a significant role in social, and by extension political, matters, there was always a clear distinction between the temporal power of rulers and the religious authority of the clergy (who are often called *ulama*, meaning "scholars").

Under Khomeini, fellow high-ranking ayatollahs were silenced as political power shifted to a single, autocratic source of authority. Through his previously obscure and controversial ideology of *wilayat al-faqih*

(Rule by the Jurisprudent), Khomeini sought to place the executive powers of the state within a single living cleric: himself. This meant that the traditional system in which believers chose which marja to follow was supplanted by an environment in which political power often outweighed religious qualifications.

Even though the majority of ulama (including Sistani) have stood against wilayat al-faqih, the economic and political role that postrevolutionary Iran has played in the Shia world has increased the status and role of Iran's Supreme Leader. And even though the current occupant of that office, Ayatollah Ali Khamene'i, is not even a Grand Ayatollah (the Iranians changed their constitution in 1989 to allow for this political appointment), his picture can be found hanging in the private homes of pious Iranian, Lebanese, and Iraqi Shias across the region.

To be Shia, of course, does not mean to automatically be against Sunnis, and vice versa. The vast majority of Muslims do not even give a second thought to their friendship with a member of a different sect, the way that an American Catholic would not think twice about associating with an American Protestant. Even on the violent-extremist front, Iran has been happy to support Sunni militant groups like Hamas and the Palestinian Islamic Jihad just as it has supported the Shia group Hezbollah in Lebanon. And after the July 2006 war between Hezbollah and Israel, many Sunni Arabs have warmed up to Iran, which provided the Lebanese militia with the thousands of missiles it lobbed on the Jewish State during that thirty-three-day campaign—the enemy of my enemy is my friend. At the same time, Sunnis have been fighting Sunnis, and Shias have been fighting Shias in postwar Iraq, a fact that only points to the conflict's jarring nuances.

One thing that must be noted about Sunni and Shia differences are the stories one rarely hears about in the West: the mutual respect harbored by the vast majority of believers in both sects. Most Muslims, as individuals, care little about doctrinal and historical differences, and they merely want to live in peace. Alas, the region's unstable history, along with its difficult geographic makeup, has forced a number of its inhabitants to live in a state of perpetual conflict.

1

THE THREE CATALYSTS

On the west side of Martyr's Square in Beirut, a plaza built to commemorate the victims of Ottoman-Turkish repression, stands a massive white tent housing the mausoleum of assassinated Lebanese prime minister Rafik Hariri. Hariri, a Sunni real estate magnate who earned his billions in Saudi Arabia, made his political name crusading against Syria's ubiquitous presence in his country. He was killed in a car explosion attributed to the Syrian regime on February 14, 2005, becoming a martyr for thousands of pro-Western Sunnis in Lebanon.

A work in progress, the makeshift mausoleum looks like a tent pitched for a high-class catering event; here today, gone tomorrow. But years after being erected it still stands, if only as a reminder that Lebanon, as a nation divided among Christian, Muslim, and other sects, is and perhaps will always be, a work in progress.

Lying in the vast tent, which is empty save for some oversized photos of Hariri and his political foot soldiers, one finds a flower-covered sarcophagus that displays a framed, smiling picture of the charismatic leader. Just to the left of the tomb, a puzzling sight: a massive portrait of Hariri stands in the prayer anteroom, while a man, a Sunni Muslim, kneels and prostrates in reverence before the late prime minister's image.

But to whom is this man praying, to God in Mecca, or to a dead political leader? In official Islamic theology, there is no question that such an act would be considered idolatry. Yet in many ways this sacrilege embodies the challenges of Islam and the sectarian divisions it has harbored since its birth in seventh-century Arabia. Islam from its very beginnings has been a religion of temporal leaders, charismatic individuals who have split the community of the faithful into innumerable and often conflicting camps. Though Hariri was only an elite politician in a largely secular movement, he might as well have been divine, a modern-day saint.

Lebanon is a microcosm of the Middle East. With its abundant sects, factions, and leaders, it is marked by hardened identities that are passed down from generation to generation. A Sunni's family will always be Sunni. But just as important, the partisans of any given leader will often hand down such allegiances to their children. Hariri's son, Saad Hariri, is already the symbol of his father's legacy; his picture can be found plastered alongside that of the elder Hariri throughout the bustling neighborhoods of West Beirut.

Robert Fisk, in his epic *Pity the Nation*, writes of "powerful feudal chieftains whom the Lebanese would describe as 'honoured families' ... Every community, every tribe, had produced its leader."[1] As we have witnessed since 2003, Fisk could have been talking about Iraq. Whether speaking of Muqtada al-Sadr, the leader of Iraq's Mahdi Army, whose followers he inherited from his father (Sadiq al-Sadr) and father-in-law (Muhammad Baqir al-Sadr); or of Abdul Aziz al-Hakim, who borrowed his legacy from his brother (Muhammad Baqir al-Hakim) and their father (Muhsin al-Hakim), it is individual, charismatic leadership that has given birth to faction after violent faction in Iraq. During times of profound crisis, the people may look to larger-than-life individuals for both religious and political guidance.

To be sure, this power of charismatic leaders is nothing new to the world. In the Korean Peninsula, the practice of attributing divine-like qualities to men is found in the North Korean leaders' cult of personality, as well as in the veneration of some business leaders of the South. In the United States, where people are proud to live in a country of "laws, not men," charismatic leaders have still surfaced, from fringe demagogues such as David Koresh, to Christian televangelists like Benny Hinn. Mainstream political figures, from Franklin Roosevelt, to Ronald Reagan, to Barack Obama, have leveraged their charismatic appeal to inspire confidence and profound loyalty among their staunchest supporters. Even within the Jewish tradition, arguably the most legalistic among the monotheistic faiths, some Chasidic movements venerate their spiritual leaders. Such is the case with Rebbe Nachman, an eighteenth-century mystic, whose grave in the Ukraine is visited in pilgrimage by tens of thousands of devoted followers every Rosh Hashanah.

In early Islam, the tradition of venerating individuals has been a key but seldom discussed historical component. In centuries past, Central Asia, which was once a wild region on the periphery of the Islamic caliphate, hosted a slew of self-proclaimed messiahs who were loosely attached to mystical Sufi sects or quasi-Shia beliefs. These fearless leaders would often rise up in revolt against the state, backed by devoted fellowships made up of newly converted Manicheans, Buddhists, and Hindus.

Even in Sunni Islam, which does not adhere to the Shia belief in Imams (i.e., infallible religious leaders), schools of jurisprudence often emerged in the name of enlightened scholars, the ideas of whom followers would be willing to defend to the death. Today, there are four such schools of Sunni jurisprudence—Hanafi, Maliki, Shafi and Hanbali— each named after their respective founder. In the ninth century, during the height of Islam's Golden Age, there were hundreds such schools, each fueled by individuals claming to know the path to juridical truth.

This concept of charismatic leaders has been one hallmark of sectarian divisions from the earliest beginnings of the Muslim faith. Yet the trend could not result in any significant levels of violence without adding a second ingredient, or catalyst, as I like to call it. This second catalyst is the breakdown of state authority. Whenever a state has been too weak to enforce its particular vision of Islam upon the populace, militant leaders have been able to rise up and challenge the status quo. When there is no anarchy, it hardly matters whether different factions disagree on religious or political issues—the state has the final say. When there is no state, the country at hand quickly turns into a contested territory where competing factions and religious movements are free to duke out their differences in the effort of establishing political control.

To the charismatic leadership and the breakdown of state power we can add a third and most important catalyst: the geopolitical battles of larger nations. These are the outside interests that play the role of puppet master in local-level, proxy conflicts. They are the great regional powers, which supply arms, money and religious legitimacy to those factions who are out to do their dirty work on the ground. These regional, geopolitical interests are the ultimate protagonists of the sectarian conflicts of Middle Eastern history, since without them it would have been difficult to imagine the levels of carnage that the Sunni-Shia conflict has inspired.

These three catalysts of sectarian violence, (1) the power of charismatic leaders, (2) the breakdown of state authority, and (3) the geopolitical battles of larger nations, by no means comprise an exhaustive list. There are countless historical factors that have contributed to sectarianism, some unique to particular time periods and the societies in which they emerged. But these three trends have proven to be most crucial and consistent in fomenting sectarianism in places like Iraq, Lebanon and throughout the rest of the Middle East, and they are therefore the focus of this book.

Because Sunni-Shia violence has resurfaced time and again, it may be tempting to view it as a result of a timeless grudge between communities of the faithful; one that can never be fully understood by outsiders, let alone mitigated. But in fact there is hope for a resolution of the sectarian violence that is currently engulfing Iraq. Once the international community recognizes that the carnage there is a consequence of a profound power imbalance in the region—namely, the emergence of an Iranian-allied Shia government in charge of the world's third-largest oil reserves—, there is hope of stopping the bleeding. So long as the problem is handled with purely tactical solutions, however, such as increased troop levels or ramped up training of Iraqi security forces; and so long as the Sunni-Shia conflict is relegated to the studies of psychology or theology, or other feeble attempts at reading the hearts and minds of combatants; the solution to Iraq's sectarian violence will remain elusive.

While U.S. policymakers have thus far failed to recognize the three catalysts of sectarian conflict, the region's political leaders have always been aware of the forces at play. During the Lebanese civil war militants understood the importance of charismatic leadership and knew how power and authority could be transmitted from one generation to the next. In 1977, when the rivalry between Christian militia leaders Pierre Gemayel and Suleiman Franjieh reached fever pitch, it was their sons, who, as heirs to their parents' political legacy, engaged in the bloodiest fighting. One day Gemayel's son Bashir ordered a group of gunmen into rival Tony Franjieh's home to kill the young leader, but only after brutally murdering his wife and baby in front of him—the bloodline had to end.[2]

In Iraq, intra-Shia rivalry has taken its share of lives. Just one day after the United States took Baghdad on April 9, 2003, Muqtada al-Sadr's partisans brutally murdered the son of the late Ayatollah Abu al-Qasem al-Khoei. Apparently Muqtada had not forgotten the feud between his uncle and the late Khoei, both of whom were high-ranking clerics.

This problem of conflicting family lines seems to be as old as time, but it became particularly intense after the rise of Islam in the seventh century. Whenever a dynasty took hold of a Middle Eastern empire in centuries past, it often did so, not only in the name of a particular belief, but out of loyalty to a particular person. The most powerful Muslim dynasties in the region's history—the Umayyads, Abbasids, Seljuks, and Ottomans—were all named after particular families, each of which traced its ancestry to an eponymous individual; revered men such as Umayya, Abbas, Seljuk, and Osman were remembered and honored long after their deaths. It is only apt, then, that the name Shia is short for *Shi'at 'Ali*—the Party of Ali. (Ali was the son-in-law of the Prophet Muhammad and the ideological father figure of the Shia sect.)

In 656 the first *fitna*, or Islamic civil war, was fought between Ali and his partisans on one side and those calling themselves the Party of Uthman—again, named after an individual—on the other. This war between the political ancestors of the Shia and the Sunni was fought in what is now Iraq, a land that has been at the conflict's center from the very beginning.

The second catalyst—a breakdown in state authority—can be thought of as the environment that makes room for the first catalyst to emerge in the first place. For violence to take place on a massive scale and for dueling factions to arise and credibly challenge the status quo, the state has had to lack the proper tools to quell insurrections. This is a position that Iraq has often found itself in, not only after the 2003 invasion but also during long and formative stretches of time in the country's history.

When looking at ethnic and sectarian conflict throughout the world, scholars have found that the lack of a strong central government has often led to some of the most violent episodes in factional war. If a government strong enough to keep mutual fears at bay is in place, it matters less whether two groups of people "have always hated each other," as the adage goes. What matters is how each group perceives the threat coming from a rival clan, ethnic group, or religious sect, and the less central authority there is to keep the peace, the more acute the mutual fears become.

The Middle East has been especially vulnerable to this catalyst of state chaos. While Europe has been divided into various small, warring states since medieval times, the Middle East has been characterized for most of its history by massive, overreaching empires. Given the inherent difficulties in maintaining order throughout large expanses of land, vacuums of state power have been the norm in the region, rather than the exception. And these power vacuums have only facilitated challenges from ambitious individuals rallying their followers around a promise of one religious awakening after another.

To be sure, Europe also experienced its share of large-scale sectarian violence, most notably between Catholics and Protestants during the Thirty Years' War (1618–48). But Europe was different in two critical ways. Unlike the Middle East during the early stages of Islam, seventeenth-century European states were fighting over what were then already established branches of Christianity, namely Roman Catholicism, Lutheranism, and Calvinism. That is, European rulers were not warring to fashion a new faith after themselves, so the outcome of a singular conflict, and the defeat of a political leader, could never be expected to drive any particular Christian branch to extinction. And while honest prayer and holy war did take place, the thousands of mercenaries who pillaged the German countryside during the Thirty Years' War were less concerned with seeking martyrdom than they were with prompt payment in gold, beer, and women.

In the Middle East, plunder was also important, but the best fighters were often the most devoted, as political leaders usually doubled as religious figures (it was not uncommon, for example, for a warlord to refer to himself as the next Mahdi, or Messiah.) The stakes in the Middle East were always higher, as a war could signal a change in course for the entire budding religion. This made postwar accommodation between belligerent factions all the more difficult.

Eventually, sectarian violence diminished in Europe, so that by the mid-1800s only periodic episodes of Protestant-on-Catholic violence are noted, and these were usually expressions of discontent with the Catholic Habsburg Empire. By then, Germans, Italians, Hungarians, and other European peoples were each clamoring for a nation-state—a political entity based less on religion than on ethnicity and a perceived common culture. The nation-state concept was ultimately exported to the Middle East by overzealous European powers, making an already fractured region even more prone to unnecessary conflict. (More on this in the chapters to follow.)

The different trajectories of Europe and the Middle East, it should be noted, do not point to a "peaceful" Christianity and a "violent" Islam; far from it. Europeans continued to kill one another in staggering numbers on the basis of ethnicity and politics long after the Peace of Westphalia (1648) began to calm Christian sectarian tensions. This larger cycle of violence didn't let up much until 1945, when large swaths of the continent had been obliterated and left to the mercy of U.S. and Soviet leaders.

In the Middle East, a region steeped in the three catalysts, Christian factions got more than their share of sectarian blood on their hands. During the Lebanese civil war, Christian militias consistently managed to outperform their Muslim peers in their application of brutality. It isn't then that one faith inspires more violence than another; it is that the Middle East as a region is prone to a particular and unrelenting brand of sectarian conflict. This point brings us to the third and final catalyst—geopolitical battles.

The third catalyst is perhaps the most powerful and long lasting of the three. It is the spark that lights the fuse of the two others, and at the same time it is the most difficult to quell, as it is engrained in the geopolitical makeup of the Middle East. When Islam was born in the seventh century, it emerged over a backdrop of existing and unresolved regional conflicts. Empires of the east, based in Iran, and those of the west, ruled from either Egypt or Anatolia (the historic region that encompasses modern-day Turkey), had been engaged since late antiquity in a battle for regional supremacy, often under the cloak of religious disputes.

In the centuries preceding the rise of Islam, nations could take part in this struggle by converting from one dominant faith to another. Kings who accepted Christianity were in essence paying allegiance to the Roman Byzantine Empire, based in Anatolia, while those who adopted Judaism or paid tribute to Zoroastrianism would line up behind Iran. The most cynical political actors used faith as a vehicle for geopolitical struggles, and those who wanted local power knew how to play the game.

Fast-forward to the year AD 680, and the map of the Middle East shows a single, massive state. By then, the caliphate, or Muslim Empire, which based its system on the teachings of the Prophet Muhammad, had taken the region by storm, employing its military prowess, religious zeal, and promise of a more equitable global system as the wind behind its mighty sails. Many have been tempted to look back on this early Muslim state with nostalgia, thinking of it as a unified nation at peace with itself. But the map of those early centuries doesn't tell us the whole story. Multiple, competing factions vied for power *within* the Islamic state, often in the name of feuding individuals, families, and religious sects. The Islamic community, or *ummah*, was never truly cohesive.

As could have been expected, the discord within the Muslim Empire fed into the existing geopolitical rivalries, particularly the seemingly eternal east-west divisions, with Iran on one side and Anatolia- or Egypt-based states on the other. The region soon split between these eastern and western camps, as it had in pre-Islamic times, though the battles were no longer colored in expressions of Christianity versus Zoroastrianism, since Islam was now overwhelming in its dominance. Rival factions now adopted competing visions of what true Islam should be. One empire would adopt Shiism, the other would become Sunni, but the fundamental divisions continued to have more to do with political geography than with faith.

That said, the polarized Middle East didn't always break down along Sunni-Shia lines; often the divisions were based on tribal affiliation, Arab versus non-Arab disputes, and other considerations. For example, the broadly defined group known as the Party of Ali, or Alids, could often count on the discontent of non-Arabs, particularly Iranians, in pursuing their interests against the Arab ruling elites, who had inherited the military and political prowess of Muhammad's empire. Yet the basic questions of religious leadership tended to be the loudest rallying cry that brought coalitions together to fight on either side of an issue.

Between the seventh and tenth centuries most of these ideological and political battles took place in what we would now call Iraq, a land where the leaders of various Muslim factions were most active and where the second Islamic dynasty had set up its capital. As time passed, however, the importance of traditional centers of power reemerged, namely the eastern (Iran) and western (Egypt and Anatolia) camps. The official propaganda employed by these states became the Sunni-Shia conflict.

When the Fatimids, a Shia dynastic empire, took hold of Egypt and its surrounding areas in 909, the Seljuk family countered by taking Iran and Mesopotamia in 1037. In typically polarizing fashion, the Seljuks adopted a conservative Sunni mantra that was neither part of their tradition nor their personal belief system. It was simply a means of competing with the Fatimids of the west, as well as other, smaller Shia elements in the east: if you're Shia, then we'll be Sunni.

When the Sunni Ottoman Empire rose to greatness in Anatolia starting in the fourteenth century, Iran countered in the sixteenth century by establishing the Safavid Empire, a state ruled by a mystical, nonorthodox

Sufi dynasty. This dynasty, despite its own freewheeling religious beliefs, undertook the massive conversion of the country into orthodox Shiism, changing the face of Iran forever.

What the Safavid rulers personally believed when they came to power did not matter. What mattered was their ability to provide an ideological and political alternative to the dominant Ottomans. By adopting Shiism, the Safavids hoped that any and all western Shias left over from Fatimid times, particularly those in Lebanon, would more likely join forces with them and act as a fifth column of opposition in Ottoman lands. This Ottoman-Safavid rivalry overwhelmed the region well into the late 1600s.

As the geopolitical struggles played out over the centuries, Iraq was in the unfortunate position of being in the middle of it all—both geographically and politically. In more ways than one, Iraq has acted as a crossroads, a battleground for competing political and religious combatants to duke out their differences. If ever there was a perfect land in which to wage a proxy regional war, Iraq is it, and we are now witnessing the country's historic role emerge once again, with Iran, Turkey, Saudi Arabia, and Syria, all jostling and angling to steer Iraq toward their own predilection.

The Sunni-on-Shia fistfights, stabbings, and hangings that shook ninth-century Baghdad have given way to suicide bombings, mortar attacks, and shootouts with AK-47s in today's Iraq. But the story remains the same: regional powers of the east (Iran) and west (now the Sunni Arab nations) are using Iraq as a battleground, one in which personal loyalties and religious faith have come together to advance the agenda of the countries involved.

In the east, there is Iran, a massive state with an 87 percent Shia population and a self-styled role as leader of the Shia world. Today, the counterweight to Iran, or what we may call the "western" states in terms of traditional geography, are Egypt, Jordan, and Saudi Arabia. These are Sunni countries that have warned against increasing Shia and Iranian influence in the region, often purposely blurring the lines between the two. And Iraq, a country with a majority Shia population but a significant and powerful Sunni community, is the place where the east and west are again converging for a fight.

Iran now has an upper hand in the geopolitical battles. Leading up to the 2003 invasion, Iran funded and trained the major Shia groups in opposition to Saddam Hussein and was therefore prepared to place its chosen leaders in power after the fall of Saddam's Sunni regime. Iraq's leading political players, including those in the highest rungs of the U.S.-backed government, have at some point either lived in or received funding from the Islamic Republic of Iran.

Iran's advantage owes not only to the fact that Iraq is a fellow Shia-majority country but to a geopolitical connection between the two countries that goes back 2,500 years, to Iran's capture of Babylon at the hand of Cyrus the Great—Iran's "king of kings." Since then, every Iranian ruler has done everything possible to keep Iraq under his influence, and since the reign of Cyrus, at least some parts of what is now modern Iraq have been under Iranian control longer than they have been free from it. Even as late as the nineteenth century, ethnic Iranians made up the majority of Shias in Iraq, and this has not escaped Sunni critics, some of whom continue to conflate the words "Shia" with "Persian," as if the two were inseparable.

So what exactly does it mean for the Middle East to be "polarized" between eastern and western camps, Iranian and Arab, Shia and Sunni? Polarity, of course, means a state of diametrical opposition. In politics, polarity refers to the hardening of divisions between states, factions, sects, or political parties. During the Cold War, our world was bipolar, meaning it comprised two dominant poles: the United States and the Soviet Union. The narrative was one of communism versus capitalism, or Soviet-style government versus democracy. Yet at the end of the day, the fight was between America and the USSR, two countries, and not necessarily two purely ideological camps. If the United States found it most convenient to support dictators, or even work with the People's Republic of China, as it did starting in 1971, it would gladly leave the promotion of democracy by the wayside.

This, of course, is nothing new. Ideologies are, and have always been, subservient to national interests. In fact, politics itself can affect the way we understand ideology to begin with. Referring to a country as "communist" during the Cold War had less to with a judgment on how closely a country was following Karl Marx's ideology, than it did with that country's political proximity to the Soviets or the Chinese. American-backed capitalist democracies were no different. The fact that free markets and free peoples became American brands meant that states that fit one of these models naturally tended to come under the protection of the United States—a country that benefited both politically and economically from their emergence.

The same has been true with religious affiliation in the Middle East. Shia empowerment following the invasion of Iraq, which overthrew minority Sunni rule, meant Iran would have a needed ally next door. This fact wasn't lost on Iran's regional competitors. In 2004 Jordan's King Abdullah II warned of a "Shia crescent" rising from Iran, through Iraq, Syria,* and Lebanon, but he might as well have been talking about an "Iranian crescent," since Iran was the country that Arab leaders feared the most and that they expected to be at the top of any Shia-led bloc.

Speaking with Al Arabiyya television, Egyptian president Hosni Mubarak didn't parse his words: "Definitely Iran has influence on Shias. Shias are 65% of the Iraqis. ... Most of the Shias are loyal to Iran, and not to the countries they are living in."[3] While this is blatant fearmongering and anti-Shia propaganda, it becomes a self-fulfilling prophecy: Why wouldn't Arab Shias in Lebanon support Iran if their countrymen already refer to them as outsiders, "Persians"?

As the reality of a new, Shia-dominated Iraq has settled in the region, sectarian rhetoric has only intensified. In June 2008 a group of twenty-two Sunni clerics based in Saudi Arabia railed against the Shia, whom they said "sow corruption and destruction among Muslims and destabilize security in Muslim countries."[4] Later that summer, renowned Egyptian cleric and commentator Yusuf al-Qaradawi warned that Shias "are heretics and their danger comes from their attempts to invade Sunni society," opening a torrent of both praise and nervous criticism from Sunni sectors across the Middle East.[5]

---

* Syria is a Sunni-majority country, but it is ruled by a family that belongs to the Alawite sect, a branch of Islam that is marginally associated with Shiism.

Despite any differences in ideology, the Sunni-Shia divide continues to play out in political terms, and it often takes the form of Saudi or Egyptian efforts to counter Iran's growing political influence. Bahrain, which has a sizable Iranian population and is predominantly Shia, receives billions of dollars in financial and developmental support from neighboring Saudi Arabia. The Saudis hardly do this out of the goodness of their hearts. They are concerned with the prospect of increased Iranian influence in the region, and Bahrain is too close to home not to anchor it strongly in the Saudi kingdom's corner.

In this fight, Iran has attempted to reach out to the Arab street. By supporting Sunni militant groups like Hamas and the Palestinian Islamic Jihad and by using its support for the Lebanese Hezbollah, a Shia group, as a way of painting itself as the leader of opposition to Israel, Iran has been able to limit the effectiveness of Arab leaders' anti-Shia propaganda. According to a University of Maryland and Zogby International poll of 2008, the Lebanese Hezbollah's political leader, Hasan Nasrallah, Syrian president Bashir al-Assad, and Iranian president Mahmoud Ahmadinejad were the three most admired leaders in the Arab world—three figures hailing in the fabled Shia crescent.[6] The fact that these political leaders are associated with pronounced anti-Israeli rhetoric and action is hardly a coincidence; it is a consequence of a deliberate policy by Iran, the Syrian regime and Hezbollah to preempt Sunni criticism by reaching out directly to Arab populations.

While many factors have played a role in the development of the Sunni-Shia conflict, the three catalysts have been the most pronounced and long lasting. By looking at charismatic leadership, the breakdown of state authority, and geopolitical battles as the main impulses behind the Sunni-Shia conflict, we begin to observe a profound and troubling problem, one whose solution lies, not in Iraq itself, but in the ambitious states that surround it. That is, the solution to the Sunni-Shia divisions in Iraq, Lebanon, and across the region, lies not with local counterinsurgency efforts or even homegrown community education and development programs. The key lies in the balance of power of the region: so long as countries fear one another, they will use the sectarian card to pursue their national security interests. In this sense, broad and bold regional diplomacy on the part of the United States will be the only way to avert a violent escalation that could spill out beyond the borders of Iraq, a land that has been a battleground for sectarian conflict since prior to the advent of Islam, and which holds the key to regional stability in the Middle East.

2

THE BATTLEGROUND

History began in Iraq. By history, of course, I mean the beginning of writing. Archeological evidence suggests this momentous development first occurred between the Euphrates and Tigris rivers some five thousand years ago. But human ambition, illustrated by constant endeavors toward ever more complex civil organizations, did not begin with written history, and neither did the story of Iraq.

Iraq has been called the cradle of civilization. The first instances of organized farming, which in turn led to urbanization, took place in the region we call Mesopotamia, meaning the "Land between the Rivers." The Tigris and the Euphrates provided abundant nourishment for Neolithic humans, with their alluvium-rich banks offering the raw materials needed for early housing, cookware, and those sun-baked tablets that would ultimately spawn written communication.

For all the pride that such a story may inspire, it is difficult to speak of Mesopotamia as a single country, at least in the modern sense of the word. Mesopotamia, which tradition also gave it the name "Iraq" (a Semitic term that refers to a river shore), has been a collection of city-states since urbanization was invented there in the late Stone Age, and this legacy has lasted thousands of years, into the Islamic era and the present day.

Today, postwar Iraq is eerily reminiscent of itself: a collection of urban strongholds, each polarized vis-à-vis the next, yet each connected by loose economic and cultural umbilical chords that would make peace through independence a nearly insurmountable task. In early Iraq, there were about a "dozen walled cities, each circled by suburbs that stretched out for as much as six miles."[1] Each city-state and each region within the modern boundaries of Iraq always had a stake in what the others did, but mutual animosity proved time and again to be more potent than mutual need.

These circumstances have for most of Iraq's existence presented a challenge to internal peace that is of colossal, seemingly irreconcilable proportions. To make matters more difficult, Iraq's central geographic location between the empires of the east, namely ancient Iran, and the west, particularly Byzantium and later the Ottoman Empire (the forefathers of modern Turkey), has served as an ideal field for warring parties of various nations, belief systems, and ethnicities. With this eye toward geography, we begin our story of Iraq. It was in Iraq, after all, that the Sunni-Shia conflict was born. This is not a reflection of its people, who have come and gone through the ages, but of its location in the heart of a region that has constantly been at war with itself. Mesopotamia is, and has always been, a regional battleground.

The Beginnings

Iraq broke the shackles of the Stone Age and established a civilized sphere starting in the third millennium BC. This development is best captured in historian Georges Roux's brief but striking summary:

> On the foothills of Kurdistan, watered every winter by the Atlantic rains, man ceases to be a wandering hunter depending for his living upon his luck and skill and becomes a farmer attached to the small piece of land from which he obtains a regular food supply. Out of clay he builds himself a house. He invents new tools to perform new tasks. He secures in sheep and cattle a permanent and easily available source of milk, meat,

wool and hide. At the same time his social tendencies develop, for the care and defence of the land call for close cooperation. Each family probably erects its own farm, cultivates its own field, grazes its own flock and makes its own tools; but several families are grouped together and form a hamlet, the embryo of a social organization. Later other revolutions will occur: metal will replace stone, villages will grow into cities, cities will be united into kingdoms and kingdoms into empires.[2]

The urbanization of Mesopotamia came as a result of intermittent floods of the Euphrates and Tigris riverbanks, which tended to occur between April and June. This time period was both a curse and a blessing in disguise. Coming "too late for winter crops and too early for summer crops,"[3] the floods forced the locals to build canals, reservoirs, and dykes to irrigate the land when the crops needed water. The result was nothing short of a technological miracle and the beginning of a force of change that has not stopped until this day: civilization.

With the mass cultivation of crops came the division of labor. No longer was every single able-bodied person relegated to food production. The arts were born, as was the need to administer increasingly complicated urban structures. Builders, bohemians, and bureaucrats emerged, all ruled by people who gained increasing stature and importance in the administration of the newfound state. And while rule by consensus or clan chief had been the norm, urban dwellings needed kings with enough muscle to turn the wheels of progress and production. Greed, certainly older than civilization itself, found new and promising avenues for expression in a rising Iraq. The Assyrian, Babylonian and Hittite Empires came and went in various forms, using their natural wealth to supply their military ambitions.

Eventually, the decline of Mesopotamian came, and starting in about the sixth century BC, the region stopped being the center of the world and started developing into the battleground that it would eventually become—a possession to be passed around between neighboring empires. This happened for several reasons. Because the miracle of mass food production spread quickly and effectively out of Mesopotamia and the Fertile Crescent, Iraq's unique geographic charm quickly diminished. As early as the fourth millennium BC, the region's breadbasket had already been adopted as far away as the British aisles.[4] And starting in the third millennium BC, high salt contents in the soil of southern Mesopotamia made the region increasingly difficult to administer, given its diminished abundance of food. More important, what Mesopotamia lacked, and what others had, were natural, defensible borders. The openness of this cradle of civilization made for comfortable farming and manageable competition among warring city-states, but it made it impossible to confront the massive nations that would eventually dominate the region.

Not one century after the death of Sumerian king Ur-Nammu, author of the oldest surviving legal code in the world, Sumerian king Shu-Sin erected a wall between the Tigris and Euphrates. Not unlike the Great Wall of China, Shu-Sin's experiment was aimed at keeping hordes of barbarians out of his crumbling domains. But this wall was a last-ditch effort, and in many ways it represented the unique weakness that would haunt the land's inhabitants for centuries to come. The Amorites, a fellow Semitic people, were clamoring for Sumer's domains, and in the year 2004 BC, they got them.

The last great empire to stem from Mesopotamia came in the form of Babylon's reemergence, under the leadership of Nebuchadnezzar II, who pushed west to defeat the combined strength of Egypt and Israel. Jerusalem was captured and burned, its holy temple destroyed. But in 539 BC, only two decades after Nebuchadnezzar's death, Iranian king Cyrus the Great conquered Babylon and at once put an end to Mesopotamian strength in the Middle East. From that moment on, Iran was engaged in a tug of war with western empires for control over the Tigris-Euphrates river valley, a battle that Iran won more often than it lost.

The Curse of Geography

When dealing with the development of a nation or a people, geography matters, and it matters a lot. Even with the advent of modern-day weaponry, unmanned aircraft, and intercontinental ballistic missiles, a country's security outlook continues to depend in large part on the character of its own neighborhood.

During the Cold War, the United States and the Soviet Union depended on massive arsenals of nuclear-tipped missiles that could travel halfway around the world to unleash doomsday on their mortal enemy. Yet geopolitics did not cease to be a consideration. The need to access and move resources, via rail, shipping lanes, and jealously guarded airspace, forced states to continue focusing on their immediate surroundings. National security has always been tied to geography, and for better or worse, geography shows "great continuity over time."[5]

Today, global terrorism, particularly the brand practiced by al-Qaeda, has led some to believe that the world is flat. It isn't. Al-Qaeda still needs resources and friendly populations. In Iraq, it is fighting not only to kill Shias and Americans, but also to establish the geographic presence it lost when the United States invaded Afghanistan in response to the terrorist attacks of September 11, 2001. To understand a country, therefore, we need to understand its location and how that location impacts most every aspect of its existence.

Iraq, from its early beginnings, was responsive to the pull and tug of the increasingly influential powers surrounding it, and the modern lines in the sand that make up its borders betray the vulnerability written into the country's DNA. This is not to say that Iraq is unique in this experience or that this weakness could never be mitigated. The great historian Veronica Wedgwood described how Germany came to be the premiere battleground of the Thirty Years' War, though she might as well have been writing about Iraq: "Germany's disaster was in the first place one of geography, in the second place one of tradition. From remote times she had been a highway rather than an enclosure, the marching ground of tribes and armies. ... The system had long ceased to conform to any known definition of a state."[6] (This chronic geographic insecurity may help explain some of the past expansionist tendencies of both modern Germany and modern Iraq.)

The traditional great powers of the Middle East that harbored territorial ambitions in Iraq were geographic fortresses compared to Mesopotamia's wide-open valleys. Iran's Zagros mountain ranges, for one, stretch from the Persian Gulf to northern Iraq and have acted as a mighty wall to keep Iran a Persian-speaking nation for over two and a half millennia. In the south, the Zagros drop straight down to the Gulf, which itself is cut off from the country's long-standing political and social center: the Iranian Plateau. In the north, Iran's Alborz ranges hug modern-day Tehran and its surrounding areas, giving protection from the Caucasus.

The region of Anatolia, comprised of modern-day Turkey, has natural barriers that are nearly as difficult to traverse. Several western empires ("western" in this case being relative to the rest of the Middle East) have called Anatolia home. Included in the region's history are the Eastern Roman, or Byzantine Empire and, of course, the Ottoman Empire, which ruled Anatolia from 1299 until 1923.

The difference between Iran's relative continuity of society and culture and Anatolia's fractured history and disparate ruling nations is in large part a consequence of geography. While Turkey enjoys natural barriers in the northern Pontiac ranges and the southern Taurus Mountains, this barely makes for a land wall equivalent to the Zagros and Alborz ranges around Iran. More important, while the nomadic civilizations of the Central Asian steppes did not become a significant military threat for Iran until after the rise of Islam, Anatolia always found itself in the crosshairs of various advanced civilizations, from the Greeks to the Romans.

Iran was able to ward off invasion more often than not; it gained and lost considerable ground throughout its 2,500-year history, while still maintaining a relatively continuous sociocultural presence in its Persian-speaking epicenter. Even following devastating, post-Islamic invasions by Arab armies, Mongols, Afghans, and the incessant meddling of Russia and Great Britain in the modern era, Iran maintained significant cultural autonomy, leading historians to claim that Iran is a land that conquers its conquerors. Iran's modern Persian language (*Farsi*) is in fact a direct descendant of the tongue once spoken by Cyrus the Great.

In contrast to Iran and even Turkey, Mesopotamia hardly enjoyed naturally defensible borders. Aside from its northern mountainous regions in Kurdistan, Iraq has been at the mercy of its neighbors whenever it was not strong or unified enough to protect itself, something not at all uncommon given the fractional nature of Iraqi politics and the incessant meddling of external powers.

Anatolia and Iran became the two opposing poles of the Middle East is in large part because both came to develop a significant interest in expansion. Neither contained the level of irrigable land necessary to sustain the kind of large protected populace it housed, so the "resources to support an empire had to come from elsewhere."[7] Because neither side was willing to gamble the future of its access to Mesopotamia and Syria to the opposing side, long periods of hot and cold wars between empires in Iran and Anatolia came to dominate the historical landscape of the region in the first millennium AD, and in some manifestations down to the modern era.

This bipolarity between eastern and western camps began to settle in place in late antiquity, when Rome repeatedly attempted to wrest lands from Iran's Parthian Empire (c. 250 BC–AD 224) and later its Sasanian Empire (224–651). Mesopotamia was especially contested, and the Parthian city of Ctesiphon, on the banks of the Tigris, was sacked numerous times by Roman armies until the Sasanids established their capital there in 226. From that moment until the Muslim conquest in the seventh century, Iran's capital remained in Mesopotamia.

As Roman-Iranian bipolarity took hold, divisions came to be couched in overt religious language. In the first three hundred years after the death of Jesus, Christianity as a unique religion had begun to spread throughout the Roman Empire. In Anatolia, large swaths of Jewish communities, and ultimately pagan gentiles, began to take up Christianity in earnest. Finally Constantine, who would ultimately base his eastern command in the Anatolian city of Byzantium*, became the first Roman emperor to officially embrace the Christian faith. Starting in 313, he allowed the faith to spread freely and made its toleration a state policy.

Iran too had been moving toward a monotheistic mind-set. Zoroastrianism, the religion of Iran during most of its pre-Islamic history, was founded on the belief of an abstract father deity named Ahura Mazda, who reigned atop a hierarchy of six archangels and a pantheon of innu-

---

* Byzantium was later named Constantinople, and finally became Istanbul, Turkey.

merable other gods and holy entities, which included the elements and stellar bodies like the sun and the moon. While it took several centuries after the rise of the Iranian Achaemenid Empire (550 BC–330 BC) to codify this religion, by the time of the pitched Sasanid-Roman battles Zoroastrianism was an orthodoxy engrained in the Iranian court. The religion boasted an intricate system of priests and court scribes, and it became the face of Iran the way Christianity had come to represent Byzantine Rome.

Apart from Zoroastrianism, Iranian-dominated Mesopotamia hosted a large Jewish population, making pre-Islamic Iran relatively friendly territory for Judaism. Following King Nebuchadnezzar's attack on Israel in the sixth century BC, Jews had arrived en masse to Mesopotamia as Babylonian captives. After Iranian King Cyrus captured Babylon, he ordered the Jewish Temple rebuilt, and ever since the practice of Judaism became a staple of Iranian-held Iraq. Some Iranian kings persecuted Jews, while others chose to tolerate, and even embrace their activities as a favored minority.

About two thousand years ago religious schools began codifying the Jewish oral traditions on Iraqi soil. This was the rabbinic era of Judaism, which came about largely as an effort to preserve Jewish communal identity while the Jews were in exile. Following the Roman destruction of the Second Temple in AD 70, Judaism declined once again in Israel, and Mesopotamia saw increasing numbers of migrant Jews, who were settled into cities that already housed large numbers of their coreligionists. And these were no ghettos. The walled cities hosted thriving academies that bustled with scholarly fervor.

For their part, Iranian Zoroastrian beliefs provided inspiration for the development of the Jewish religion as it was being put together: Judaism's idea of heaven and hell and the belief in archangels are believed to have been taken from Zoroastrianism and became pillars of the Abrahamic religions. Later Muslim rulers would attempt to mimic, and in many ways overshadow, these Jewish metropolises of Iraq with built-to-order centers of faith such as Baghdad and Najaf.

Judaism made a presence in Arabia as well. The city of Yathrib (later called Medina) became another focal point for Judaism following the demise of the Second Temple. But in a climate of superpower rivalry between Iran and Rome, Arabian Jews could not help being pulled into the struggle. Kings who favored Judaism, including the notorious Dhu Nuwas of southern Arabia, were emblematic of the struggle for dominance over the culturally rich Arabian Peninsula.

Dhu Nuwas, ruler of Himyar, was a convert to Judaism who began a brutal persecution of Christians around 523. He ordered massacres in Najran, near modern-day Yemen, prompting Roman Emperor Justinian, a Christian, to intervene on the part of his coreligionists. As continually happens with sectarian violence, outside interests were brought to bear on the small, localized religious conflict. In this case, the systemic regional divisions between Iran in the east and Rome in the west played out like the proxy wars of the Cold War.

On Justinian's behest, Christian Ethiopia sent an expeditionary force into Najran and occupied the kingdom to protect its Christian population. Decades later, Iran intervened to oust the Ethiopians by force. Jonathan Berkey writes,

> Penetration of Arabia by the Roman and Sasanian empires, and by Christianity, Judaism, and Zoroastrianism, was always tentative, its implications and consequences always ambiguous. What, for example, did it mean to be an Arabian Jew? For Dhu Nuwas, it clearly involved struggle with both Christianity and Rome, and probably implied some alignment of interest with the Sasanian empire, itself of course the home of the largest and most vibrant Jewish community of late antiquity.[8]

Iran and Rome were certainly not always at war. Even during the decline of Sasanian power in Iran in the fourth and fifth centuries AD, when "a Roman army could usually defeat a Persian one in a set battle, or at any rate hold the Euphrates frontier securely,"[9] Rome was all too willing to make peace with a weaker opponent. Whenever Rome and Iran were concerned will lesser threats, such as those posed by nomadic incursions and rebellions, they were happy to draw treaties and focus on internal control.

These were periods of relative peace, but the cold war persisted.

When Sasanian Iran made a comeback in the early seventh century, it undertook an offensive of dramatic proportions. The Iranians took Jerusalem and "seized the relic believed to be the True Cross of Christ."[10]After ordering a mass deportation of Christians, they brought Jews back into the city for resettlement as a show of force. Iran raided large swaths of Anatolia and took hold of Egypt. But Byzantium soon countered with an offensive of its own, and the status quo ante returned. The eastern empire of Iran and the western empire of Rome were locked in a timeless sectarian battle, one that engulfed the entire region and set a precedent for the conflicts of the Islamic era.

3

THE MESSAGE AND
THE MESSENGERS

Just south of Iraq, in the Arabian Peninsula and in the shadows of the Sasanid-Byzantine rivalry, there was a vacuum of power, ideas, and regional gravitas. In this context a new figure emerged out of Arabia with a message that united the disparate tribes of the peninsula and brought a cultural and religious revolution to the world.

Muhammad, who according to Islam is the last monotheistic prophet, was born around the year 570 into the dominant Quraysh tribe of Mecca, in the Arabian Peninsula. Specifically, Muhammad was part of the Banu Hashim, or Hashimite, clan. By the age of six, he had lost both of his parents, and by eight, he had also lost the grandfather who had cared for him after he was orphaned. Muhammad was soon taken in by his uncle Abu Talib, a successful merchant who played a central role in the upbringing of this righteous and respected member of Meccan society.

In pre-Islamic times, Mecca, a city in the Hijaz region of eastern Arabia, was critical to the economic and spiritual life of the peninsula, as it held the Ka'ba (the Cube), a stone and marble structure that housed the idols and religious symbols of the day. Believers from around the region would arrive yearly to commemorate their unique gods. Even the likenesses of Jesus and the Virgin Mary were placed inside the sacred structure. As Reza Aslan notes, when Muhammad made his triumphant return to Mecca as the Prophet of Islam and ordered the Ka'ba idols smashed to pieces, the reliefs of Jesus and Mary were the only two spared.[1]

Because Muhammad was born into a family of merchants, his exposure to monotheism went beyond what was practiced in the Arabian Peninsula. His caravan trips to Syria likely exposed him to the large Christian community there, and his cousin Waraqa, a member of an Abrahamic cult, provided a more intimate connection to the antipagan teachings of Judaism and Christianity. Eventually, Waraqa converted to Christianity and provided Muhammad with a boost of religious support.

From early in life, Muhammad was an individual of exceptional intelligence and perceptive abilities. By most accounts, he was a quiet, gentle, and empathetic merchant. His kindness was even extended to animals, something not customary in the region at the time. His sensitive and contemplative nature guided him through existential questions as his faith developed over the years.

Muhammad's mission started around AD 610, when he began to proselytize. As had the prophets of many prior traditions, Muhammad assumed his role following an event of profound contemplation. For days on end, Muhammad would dwell in a cave on Mount Hira, near Mecca, to meditate and escape from the worldly concerns of merchant life. During one of these contemplative episodes the angel Gabriel is said to have visited him. The angel told Muhammad to read from a passage of revelation he placed before him. Though it is said that Muhammad could not read, the angel literally pressed him, almost suffocating him, until Muhammad finally spoke:

> Recite: In the name of your Lord who created
> He created man from an embryo
> Recite: And your Lord, most exalted
> Who teaches by the pen
> Teaches man what he never knew (Qur'an 96:1–5)

This verse began Muhammad's life as a prophet.

As he upset the status quo with increasing talk of a single god, human equality and empathy for the poor, Muhammad was forced to leave Mecca for Yathrib. This event, called the *Hijra* (Emigration), took place in 622 and marks the beginning of the Muslim calendar. While Muhammad eventually drew up a treaty with the Meccans, he did not return to the city in full glory until 630, when most Meccans converted to his new religion, Islam. In 632 Muhammad returned again to make his farewell pilgrimage to the sanctuary of the Ka'ba, which was then no longer a pantheon, but Islam's holiest site.

Muhammad's brand of monotheism spread like wildfire throughout the Middle East, in part because of the general displeasure with both Roman and Iranian dominance, but also owing to the fighting prowess of Islamic fighters, who conquered vast swaths of land in the name of the state that the Prophet Muhammad had founded. Although the topic of violent conversion has been a source of controversy in the West, few would expect other empires to have spread entirely peacefully. Still, this is the high standard that is often set by both detractors and revisionist supporters of the early Muslim state. Islam spread like any other empire of the time—through both violence and diplomacy.

Violence, however, was nothing new in the experience of monotheism. In 435 Christian Emperor Theodosius II issued an edict "requiring the destruction of any pagan temples and shrines still remaining intact, and the purification of their sites by setting up a cross."[2] Pagans who resisted faced death. Jonathan Berkey explains how early Christian conversions likely inspired the Muslim campaigns a few centuries later: "The growing level of Christian hostility is surprising, as late antique paganism shared much with the new religion of Christianity. ... The emphasis on conversion suggests once again the growing importance to the men and women of late antiquity of formal expressions of religious identity. In that may lie Christianity's greatest legacy to the world which, in the seventh century, Islam inherited."[3]

This is not to say that conversion to Islam happened automatically. Parts of the emerging empire did not convert to Islam until two centuries following their conquest. This was because, contrary to common perceptions in the West, Muslim generals did not always force the conversion of the peoples they had subjugated. Instead, they provided incentives, such as nontaxation and access to government work, as the driver behind the largely voluntary shift toward Islam.[4]

An Empire Divided

After the death of the Prophet in 632, the future of this rising Arab empire hung in the balance. Who would succeed Muhammad was important enough, but something more profound than mere personalities was at stake. In Middle Eastern politics, and no less in the Arabian Peninsula, tribe and clan affiliations were of utmost concern to believers, and deciding who would rule would be the critical question.

Muhammad belonged to the Quraysh tribe, so would the next ruler of Islam also hail from the Quraysh? Would authority rest within the Hashimites in particular? These were no small matters, given the fact that under Muhammad the Islamic state had already grown to control of much of the Arabian Peninsula and enjoyed treaties with Iranian-ruled Yemen and neighboring tribes. Leadership was no longer just a question of piety and personality. It was a matter of the state.

We know that immediately following Muhammad's death his cousin and son-in-law Ali, along his wife Fatima, attended the washing of Muhammad's body for burial. As this was happening, Abu Bakr, one of the Prophet's most trusted companions, was elected in an ad hoc council, or *shura*, to be the Prophet's successor—the new Commander of the Faithful. Ali had been under the impression that he was to succeed Muhammad. Shia sources say that during Muhammad's Farewell Pilgrimage to Mecca, the Prophet stopped the caravan midway to proclaim Ali his successor: "Of whomsoever I am lord, then Ali is also his lord. O God! Be Thou the supporter of whoever supports Ali and the enemy of whoever opposes him."[5]

For many Sunni scholars, Ali's youth and lack of experience at the time justified his exclusion from the assembly (Ali was in his early thirties at the time of Muhammad's death). Furthermore, Sunni scholars have proclaimed that, in the spirit of Islam, the House of the Prophet did not have to be revered as inherently endowed with divinity. It was the message, not the messenger himself, who was to be exalted.

For those who followed Ali, it became difficult not to reject Abu Bakr's rise. After all, Abu Bakr was aging and could not have been expected to be a serious leader for long, while the way in which he was selected—behind the backs of Ali and the Prophet's family—reeked of foul play.

Regardless of what transpired, we can conjecture that personal animosity between Ali and Abu Bakr played at least some role in the succession controversy and the divisions that would continue throughout the centuries. There is an oft-told story about Aisha, a favored wife of the Prophet, which lends some clues. The "Story of the Necklace" recounts how, during a caravan trip, Aisha had left the encampment to look for her lost necklace. As she did this, the caravan left without her, and she ended up stranded in the desert for hours. A childhood friend named Safwan, who was passing by, finally picked her up and took her on his camel to catch up with the caravan.

Once Aisha caught up, rumors and whispers brought doubt to her story, and some outright accused her of committing adultery with Safwan. Ali, for one, suggested that given the chatter, it would be appropriate for the Prophet to divorce her. Abu Bakr, who was Aisha's father, did not take too kindly to this suggestion, and it is possible that his grudge lasted until well after Muhammad's death. At the end of the day, the Prophet received a revelation that Aisha was without fault, and he ordered the accusers lashed.

Beginning with Abu Bakr, each leader who succeeded Muhammad as head of the Islamic state was known as the *Khalifat Rasul Allah*, or 'Deputy to the Messenger of God.' A *khalifa*, or caliph, represented the temporal authority of the empire, along with a measure of religious leadership (at least during the early centuries of Islam). Some, including Abu Bakr's successors Umar and Uthman, took the title of *Khalifat Allah* (deputy of God), essentially lifting themselves to prophet-like status. This did not go over well with many later Muslim historians, who continued to stress the human and fallible nature of the office of the caliphate.[6]

Despite the foibles associated with the office, the first four leaders to succeed the Prophet are considered to have possessed, at least by Sunni accounts, particularly high judgment, piety, and devotion to the true principles of Islam. These four Rightly Guided Caliphs (al-Khulafa al-Rashidun), as they came to be known, were Abu Bakr, Umar, Uthman, and, finally, Ali. While Abu Bakr directly appointed Umar, the two others were selected through the consensus of a tribal council, very much in Arab tradition.

In many ways, Abu Bakr's brief term (632–634) was an interregnum, a transition between the Prophet's charismatic leadership and the temporal power of the new empire under Umar, the second caliph. Umar oversaw the expansion of the Muslim state to new heights, waging wars in Syria, Egypt, Mesopotamia, and Iran, and reaching the holy city of Jerusalem in 637. He changed the map of the Middle East and appeared invincible until his assassination at the hand of an Iranian slave in 644. (He was the first in a long line of caliphs who faced premature death.)

The selection of Uthman, who, like the other two caliphs, was a member of the Quraysh tribe but not the Banu Hashim clan, left something to be desired for the partisans of Ali. Though Ali had advanced his own candidacy to succeed Umar, the cards were consistently stacked against him owing to lingering doubts about his qualifications and the general desire by council members to keep the caliphate away from the Banu Hashim, if only to avoid a familial succession. Ironically, however, Uthman's reign soon led the Muslim empire down the road of dynastic rule.

Uthman was a member of the powerful Umayya family of the Banu Abd Shams clan. Since pre-Islamic times, the Umayyads had fought the Hashimites in a long-standing feud. So when Muhammad began his prophecy, Abu Sufyan, an Umayyad, led the pagan opposition to the Prophet's message in Mecca.[7] When Mecca was finally Islamicized, Muhammad did not cast away the Umayyads, an entrenched and elite family, but brought them in to put their political and economic contacts to work for the new state.

When Syria was taken from Byzantium in 636, Yazid, son of Abu

Sufyan, was made its governor. From Damascus, where the Umayyads enjoyed strong clan ties, the family launched a systematic campaign to consolidate power under the new Muslim order. It didn't seem to matter to them that paganism was out and monotheism was in. What mattered was achieving a system in which the Umayyads, and not anyone else, was at the top of the tribal pecking order.

The Umayyads' consolidation of power had been decades in the making before they finally took hold of the caliphate in the year 661, undoing the process of consultation and adopting a monarchical dynasty within their own family. When Uthman was elected caliph in 644, he still represented the spirit of Rightly Guided leadership. But while he had overseen critical developments of the faith, with the expansion of Muslim architecture and the consolidation of the Qur'an's chapters into their present form, he also set a trap, unwittingly say historians, for the demise of the electoral council.

Under Uthman's auspices, members of his fellow Umayya clan were given high posts, including governorships in Egypt, Kufa, and Basra. While this gave disproportionate power to the Umayyads, Uthman's otherwise prudent concern with territorial overreach proved to be the downfall of his reign.

Muslim generals, who had been looking to exploit military gains by having land appropriated to them, protested the limitations on expansion that Uthman established. His new policy initiatives were aimed at curbing the waste associated with a permanent Muslim campaign of expansion, as well as better managing the lands that the empire already held. Despite the prudence of these policies, there was little Uthman could do to placate opposition amid charges of excessive nepotism or to mitigate the anger of ambitious generals who did not want to accept the new limits on conquest. A movement of rebellion quickly grew and even included Abu Bakr's own son. The opposition finally struck in Egypt, where it besieged and killed Uthman in 656.

The death of Uthman marked the hardening of two camps in early Islam—a polarization of tribal and political affiliation, but not yet representing a religious divide. On one hand, those who believed that Uthman's death had been a punishable, legal transgression sought to bring the killers to justice before settling on a successor. This camp, which came to regard the Prophet's son-in-law Ali as the culpable party, was known as *Shi'at 'Uthman*, the Party of Uthman. On the other side of the argument were the rebels, who, considering Uthman a transgressor of the faith and believing that his death was a just and rightful punishment, favored the swift election of Ali as the next caliph. This was the Shi'at 'Ali, which today are simply known as the Shia.

The battle lines between the Party of Ali and the Party of Uthman were drawn in Iraq. Aisha, in her stalwart opposition to Ali, accused him of conspiring to assassinate Uthman and went in person to Basra, in modern-day Iraq, to raise an army against the newly elected caliph. Determined to fight for his hard-won seat of power, Ali left for Kufa, also in Mesopotamia, where he raised an army of his own. This series of events is known as the Great Fitna (Time of Trial)—the Muslim civil war.

In December 656, just outside of Basra, Ali and Aisha met in the Battle of the Camel, named for the animal Aisha rode during the fight. Ali won decisively and banished Aisha back to the Hijaz, but the fitna was far from over. Earlier in 656, Ali had placed the seat of the caliphate in Kufa, where Arabs from the peninsula had begun to stream in for the spoils of the rich Mesopotamian lands. Southern Iraq soon grew to be a center of Shia learning and leadership, and today Shias from all over the world make pilgrimage to cities such as Karbala and Najaf.

The Umayyads, whose center of power lay in Damascus, quickly moved to undermine Ali and wrest the caliphate from him. They met him in the Battle of Siffin (657), which ended inconclusively, with a call for arbitration. Ironically, it was not the Umayyads, but members within Ali's own army, that dealt the final blow to the Prophet's son-in-law. The Kharijites were a small faction of malcontent Alids who, feeling slighted by Ali's acceptance of arbitration, walked out on the caliph and eventually murdered him in January 661.

The Umayyad caliphate lasted from the death of the last Rightly Guided Caliph, Ali, until an insurrection mounted from eastern Iran brought it to an end in 750. One of the lasting legacies of the Umayya is their role in the most formative event in the development of Shia identity. Acting as the antagonist in the Battle of Karbala (680) against Alid forces, the Umayyad system came to represent the essence of what Shia doctrine desires to combat through its revolutionary appeal.

After Ali's death, the Shi'at 'Ali chose his son Hasan as a natural successor, the next caliph to be based in Kufa. Parallel to Hasan's claim, however, was that of Muawiya, son of Yazid, then the Umayyad governor of Syria. Muawiya, as a member of the Shi'at 'Uthman, naturally fought to keep the caliphate to himself and the Umayyads. As Muawiya prepared for battle against Hasan, Ali's son capitulated, seeing himself hopelessly outnumbered and outmaneuvered. It appears that the Umayyads had bribed several officials in Kufa, a place that would time and again let the Shia down in their quest for control over the empire. In the year 669, with the Umayyads firmly in power, Hasan perished, presumably by poison. But Alids didn't give up, and Hasan's younger brother Husayn took over his role as commander of the Shia faithful.

The title the Shia gave to Ali and his sons was that of *Imam*. The Imamate, according to the Party of Ali, was to represent a mantle of leadership, which, not unlike that of the Prophet, was based on the assumption of infallible judgment, character, and knowledge. The Imams, hailing from the Banu Hashim, but particularly the line of Ali and his wife Fatima (the daughter of the Prophet), represented a kind of divine hereditary succession through which generations of Muslims would keep alive the Prophet's charismatic authority in their own times.[8] According to Shias, Ali was the first Imam, and Hasan and Husayn were the second and third, respectively.

When Muawiya died in 680, he appointed his son Yazid I (named after Muawiya's father), to lead the caliphate in Damascus. Husayn, still claiming the title for himself and his family, set off from the Hijaz to the city of Karbala, in Mesopotamia, where he met Yazid's forces in battle for control of the empire.

Husayn is said to have stopped in Kufa to increase his numbers and supplies. He had been warned against the waffling nature of the city's inhabitants but nevertheless took seriously their pledge to fight alongside him. The people of Kufa, however, disappointed yet again, refusing to come out and join Husayn. Many locked their doors to avoid the leader to whom they had sworn allegiance.

In the running narrative of Shiism, the Kufans of the seventh century deserve particular scorn. Having turned their back on a battle of ultimate importance, they represented a dark stain on the pride of the Shia. During the Iranian Revolution, the phrase "We are not Kufis!" became a symbol of bravery and determination against the shah, the Yazid of the day. For the Shia, metaphors carrying the name "Yazid" (an oppressor), "Kufi" (a coward), and "Husayn" (a revered martyr) continue to carry potent meaning, particularly in times of armed combat. To fight and die for one's faith, a Shia may say, is like fighting alongside Imam Husayn in the Battle of Karbala.

The events at Karbala took place over ten days, with the death of Husayn coming on the tenth of the first Muslim month of Muharram, which is the holy day of *Ashoura*. Ashoura, literally meaning "the tenth," likely originated from the Jewish holy day of Yom Kippur, which also falls on the tenth (Hebrew: *asor*) of the first month of the Jewish calendar. Like Yom Kippur, Ashoura was designated a fast day by Muhammad, though later, following his rift with the Jewish tribes of Arabia, the Prophet made Ramadan into a month of obligatory fasting, and left Ashoura merely as a voluntary fast. For the Shia, however, the day of Ashoura came to represent the formation of their unique community, ready and willing to stand up to the perceived injustice of impious rule.

In the days leading up to the tenth of Muharram, Husayn's camp, which included seventy-two men, along with women and children, was cut off from the Euphrates by Yazid's forces. The caliph had ordered the submission of Husayn on pain of death, and Karbala was to be the decisive battle. At midday on Ashoura, Husayn is said to have gone into his wife's tent and picked up his six-month-old son, Ali al-Asghar, who was then nearly dead from thirst and hunger. Taking him outside alone onto the battlefield, he yelled to the caliph's troops, pleading with them to have mercy on the little one and allow him a drink of water.

For a moment, goes the story, the opposing army was visibly moved, and sobs could be heard echoing across the horizon as the pale baby's open mouth revealed a dry, cracked tongue. But in an effort to bring his troops into line, the Umayyad commander ordered his best archer to take aim and fire. Suddenly, an arrow flew straight through the baby's neck, drenching his father with the blood of the House of Muhammad. There was to be no mercy.

By sunset all of Husayn's men had been martyred, and the Imam's white stallion returned to the women's encampment alone, a sign of his master's fate. It is said that Husayn was trampled numerous times by enemy horses, struck with dozens of arrows, and slashed by Umayyad swords. And as Husayn, the grandson of the Prophet, knelt to pray one last time before death, his head was severed with the thumping blow of a sword.

Days later, the heads of seventy-two martyrs were put up on spears and taken along with the women and children to Damascus, where they were handed over as tribute to the Caliph Yazid. But Ali's lineage did not die in Karbala, as Husayn's son, Ali Zaynu al-Abidin*, had been too weak to fight and had thus remained back in the camp.

Like Jesus contemplating his execution at Gethsemane, it is said that Husayn knew the fate that awaited him at Karbala. Yet rather than field a large enough army, he sought a change in the hearts and minds of the nascent Muslim community. A win on the battlefield can always be outdone by a greater army, one Shia historian noted, but "a victory achieved through suffering and sacrifice is everlasting and leaves permanent imprints on man's consciousness."[9]

Pilgrims from Iran, Lebanon, and other parts of the Muslim world have traveled to Karbala whenever the political situation has allowed them to do so, paying homage at the shrine that sprung up in Husayn's honor. And every year, in the Shia passion play (*ta'ziya*), pious mourners donning black recount the agony of thirst, hunger, and pain at Karbala. Many beat their chests and sob in remembrance of their martyred Imam. "Ya, Husayn!" they call out, a few even hitting their heads with swords or flagellating their backs with chains and whips, wishing that they could somehow turn history on its head and fight alongside their martyred

---

* Imam Zaynu al-Abidin is a source of pride for Iranian Shias. He is believed to be the son of a Persian princess, who handpicked Imam Husayn for marriage.

leader.

In 2003 Iraqi militiaman Muqtada al-Sadr called on the followers of his father, the late Ayatollah Sadiq al-Sadr, to commemorate the ritual fortieth day (*Arba'in*) after the mourning of Ashoura with a historic pilgrimage to Karbala. Such processions had been banned by the twentieth century's Sunni Yazid, Saddam Hussein. But now he was gone. At that moment, Muqtada picked up the mantle of leadership from his dead father and started a revolutionary movement that was as much about fighting a perceived enemy as it was about finally giving a voice to the Shia in the land that gave birth to their faith.

4

FAULT LINES

On March 25, 816, Caliph Ma'mun emerged from his private counsel in the distant city of Marw, in the eastern Iranian province of Khorasan. He had chosen a successor, a new face to shake up the relatively new but unstable caliphate. The Umayyads had long been defeated. Since 750, the Abbasids, a new dynasty, had been leading the Muslim Empire, with the newly built city of Baghdad as their seat of power.

Back in Baghdad anything but calm awaited Ma'mun's return. Five years prior, Ma'mun had taken the caliphate by force of arms from his brother Amin when he ordered a siege of the capital "unparalleled in Islamic history, and involving blockade, bombardment of the city, famine, and hand-to-hand combat."[1] Now, the Iraqi countryside was ablaze in a sectarian war between the Party of Ali and the Abbasid family.

In Kufa and Basra, factions of Shia staged massive rebellions in support of their leaders; one of them, Ali bin Musa bin Jafar, known simply as *al-Rida* (the Chosen One), came to play a pivotal role in Ma'mun's politics and philosophy. Baghdad soon degenerated into open war, split sect by sect and fought over neighborhood by neighborhood. Ira Lapidus writes, "With the breakdown of political authority, the populace of Baghdad was exposed to gangs of thieves. . . . Houses were attacked, people were robbed or kidnapped and held for ransom. Women were not safe on the streets, while merchants and artisans were subject to extortions and the operation of protection rackets."[2]

In response to the chaos, vigilante groups emerged, armed with fundamental zeal and a call to divine order. These Sunnis would run wild through neighborhoods, shouting the slogan, "Command the good and forbid the evil!" From among them emerged Sahl ibn Salama, an iconic leader whom some today would derisively call a Wahhabi. Sahl was known to walk about with a copy of the Qur'an hanging from his neck, preaching for a religious revival. He expected his followers to abide by the literal teachings of the Prophet and not the worldly authority of the caliphs. Most of all, he expected the people to obey him.

The wealthy merchants of Baghdad, reticent to pay taxes, soon joined Sahl in the typical coalition of religious fundamentalists and moneyed interests that has resurfaced time and again throughout history. "Command the good and forbid the evil!," Sahl's men shouted before attacking bandits, the caliph's security forces, and whomever else they perceived as tainted with unbelief.

These sectarian conflicts had always plagued the fractured ummah, and the Islamic community was made up of so many disparate parts it now existed only in name. The wars were fought on multiple fronts, at times making it impossible to unravel allegiances or even the purpose for any given attack. Caliph Ma'mun, for one, faced at once an insurrection from within his family, revolts by disparate Shia branches, and the call to arms by Sahl and his fellow Sunni Traditionalists.

In the absence of a strong enough state, a wide open and dangerous market of belief soon emerged. Pious Muslims could now choose from among literally hundreds of holy men and self-proclaimed messiahs, each brandishing a unique style of Islam, and each adamant about the spiritual and political validity of his claims. Islam, after all, had not yet developed an orthodoxy, a rigid set of beliefs to differentiate believer from non-believer. The Qur'an alone did not provide a blueprint for the management of a state, let alone a massive empire, so the spiritual ground was constantly shifting under the community's feet. Different caliphs would embrace different ideas about Islam; and different revolutionaries would claim different reasons for waging an insurgency.

As Ma'mun stood on the eastern reaches of his fragile empire, he understood that a bold move was in order. To quiet the Shia disruptions, he selected the old and untested al-Rida, the Shia Imam himself, as his successor. Rida, or, as more commonly seen in the Persian, "Reza," was the grandson of the popular Imam Jafar al-Sadiq, and his ascension to the caliphate would have marked the beginning of the Shia empire the partisans of Ali had demanded for so long.

By choosing Reza to succeed him, Ma'mun was certainly taking a gamble, given the volatile relationship between the Alids and the caliphate in general. But the caliph had his own reasons for selecting an outsider. Having killed his own brother and now fighting a war on several fronts, Ma'mun needed an avenue of legitimacy outside of his own family. After announcing his succession, the caliph changed the color of his guard from Abbasid black to Alid green, minted coins bearing the Imam's name, and set off to Baghdad to end the revolt and begin a new chapter in the empire's history.[3]

Had Reza succeeded Ma'mun, the history of Sunni-Shia relations might have taken a drastic turn. Sectarianism may have given way to a middle ground, the kind that saw Shias accept the validity of the first Sunni caliphs, and Sunnis the infallibility of Ali and the Imams. Ma'mun likely wished this compromise for the sake of unity and effective governance. But it was never to be.

Reza died en route to Baghdad in the Khorasani city of Tus. Some say he was poisoned by the caliph himself, who might have realized he was offering the Shia much more than he was able to deliver. After all, his own royal family was rabidly anti-Shia, and the Alids themselves were divided over Reza's legitimacy. Yet Ma'mun is said to have been genuinely fond of the Imam, and for three days the caliph mourned at Reza's side. The Imam Reza Shrine was ultimately erected over the Shia leader's grave. It is a massive, ornate mosque that draws millions of pilgrims every year to the Iranian city that sprung up around it: Mashhad, the "Abode of Martyrdom."

Competing Claims

The Abbasid caliphate, which deposed the Umayyads in the middle of the eighth century and to which Caliph Ma'mun belonged, embodied the identity crisis that had challenged the Muslim community from the beginning. Initially inspired and fueled by frequent Alid revolts, the Abbasids were a Hashimite dynasty, that is, they hailed from the Prophet's family of Banu Hashim. And despite their embrace of Sunni Islam, they employed Shia revolutionary concepts to attain power. It is in the Abbasids that the lines between the Shia and Sunni communities are most blurred and subject to interpretation. And it is during the early Abbasid caliphate, more than at any other time, that the direction of the Sunni-Shia conflict could have changed drastically, as the example of Ma'mun and Reza suggest.

Prior to the Abbasids coming to power, there had been several failed insurrections aimed at toppling the Umayyads. The Battle of Karbala, while remembered as a singular, game-changing event in the history of Shiism, was but one in a series of actions during the seventh and early eighth centuries that had the aim of overthrowing the corrupt leaders in Damascus. But only the Abbasids, who were able to blur so many theological lines and bring so many disparate groups together in a grand coalition, were able to overpower the Umayyad state.

In 684 a group of Alid revolutionaries sought to bring the House of the Prophet front and center by propping up the candidacy of Muhammad bin al-Hanafiya, not only as an Imam, but as the messiah himself. Al-Hanafiya's followers were soon labeled "extremists" (*ghulat*) and were marginalized and crushed militarily. Yet the legacy of their chosen leader, who traced his roots back to Ali, had a lasting impact on the stream of oppositional movements taking hold within Muslim lands.

This sect of the ghulat was increasing in power and determination through the decades, and it was soon led by Ibrahim ibn Muhammad ibn Ali, a direct descendant of the Prophet's uncle Abbas. As with most revolutionary movements, it was legitimacy, rather than a specific plan for governing or religious fellowship, that provided the core of the movement's appeal.[4]

As the movement grew in power, its rhetoric became more accommodating. The multifaceted revolt movements, now led by the family of Abbas, broadened the definition of legitimate right to succession to include,
not only the direct descendants of Ali, but those of the entire the Hashimite clan. Certainly, this caused fractures within "the extremist wing of
the movement, [which] felt betrayed by this 'sell-out' to more moderate
ideas but it was necessary if the Abbasids were ever to be generally accepted as leaders of the whole community, not just a small group."[5]

Patricia Crone notes, however, that there is no evidence to suggest
that the Party of Ali saw itself as distinct and above the entire Hashimite
clan, not then at least.[6] The House of Ali, after all, obtained its legitimacy concurrently from the Prophet, his son-in-law Ali, and the Prophet's
daughter Fatima. In other words, early Shiism had begun as a broader,
undefined group of revolutionaries, and it is difficult to draw a sharp distinction between Shias who supported the Abbasids, and those who did
not.

In the region of Khorasan, the missionary call (*dawa*) of the Abbasids grew the loudest, and it was from Khorasan that the Abbasid revolution was led to victory. That region proved, as it would for centuries
to come, that it could have a disproportionate impact on the politics of
the empire. Nestled in the hills of eastern Iran and extending out into
the steppes of Central Asia, the area's Arab fighters and discontents benefited from the limited reach of imperial armies and tax burdens. This
isolation fomented a kind of frontier mentality that didn't lend itself well
to central authority. Just as important, it was in Khorasan where Arab
Muslims had most thoroughly assimilated with local society, becoming a
class of Persian-speaking Arabs, an aristocracy conquered by the imposing lands and customs of eastern Iran.

In the years directly preceding the Abbasids' victory, the Zaydis, a
group that later became an independent branch of Shiism, rebelled on
behalf of Zayd, the son of the fourth Shia Imam. The Umayyad Caliph
Hisham had killed Zayd in 740, but he left behind a son, Yahya, who fled
to Khorasan to take up the mantle of rebellion until he was also killed in
743. Those who had accepted his dawa looked for leadership and found

it in the Abbasids, who had sent their able administrators eastward to persuade the malcontents to their cause.

In a move telling of their political genius, the Abbasid revolutionaries chose Abu Muslim, a non-Arab freedman of Ibrahim ibn Muhammad (now the self-proclaimed Imam of the Abbasids), to lead the revolt in Khorasan. Apart from his aptitude, Abu Muslim was chosen "because his appointment would encourage the non-Arab Muslims of the province to take up the Abbasid cause."[7] In addition to its large and discontented Arab population, Khorasan at the time was teeming with freed slaves, making it the right place to take up a successful military insurrection.

In the summer of 747, the Abbasid revolution began in earnest near the provincial capital of Marw before moving westward. The Umayyad-Abbasid war was fought largely on Iranian soil, where discontent for the existing caliphate and the Arab ruling elite only helped the relatively small revolutionary armies swell with recruits. Iranian fighters, the ghulat, were extreme in their veneration of the Abbasid Imam. Their background was Zoroastrian, Manichean, and Buddhist; for them, faith bordered on what strict monotheists would consider idolatry, as they "professed to obey their leaders without enquiring into what constituted obedience and disobedience to God."[8]

The main battle between the Umayyads and the Abbasids occurred in March 749 near Esfahan, Iran, and by August the revolutionaries had arrived in Iraq, where a homegrown Shia insurrection was already brewing. Using his extensive network of spies and allies, Abu Muslim ensured that Abu al-Abbas, the current Abbasid Imam, was named caliph inside the Grand Mosque of Kufa. But this was only the beginning, as the sectarian and factional conflicts in Iraq continued to increase in fervor, determination, and brutality.

While brandishing itself as a Hashimite empire, the Abbasid caliphate was a far cry from most Alids' expectations for Hashimite rule. Though Abu al-Abbas branded himself an Imam and messiah, the Alids eventually came to look specifically and exclusively to the House of Ali, and not that of Abbas, for leadership. In fact, the idea that the Banu Hashim had achieved the caliphate was itself the source of the continued split. Crone explains that after the House of Abbas' success, the Abbasids brought to the forefront a simple but critical question: Why not the House of Ali? From henceforth, the Hashimites were split into two competing camps, the Shi'at 'Ali and the *Shi'at bani al-'Abbas* (the Party of the Clan of Abbas).

Soon enough, the Abbasids embraced the doctrine of the four Rightly Guided Caliphs, splitting further from the Alids and moving closer to the status quo. Shiism, to use the simple term, might have been the majority faith in the Islamic world had the Abbasids persevered in convincing the partisans of Ali that the House of Abbas was the correct source of legitimacy. But given the Alids' increasing opposition to the Abbasids, the latter were eventually pushed toward the orthodoxy of Islam: they joined, through a drawn-out process, those whom we now call Sunni.

Once in power, the Abbasids did not fail to contradict. A caliph with Alid sympathies would be succeeded by a rabid persecutor of the Shia. Baghdad, the city built by the Abbasids as the new seat of the empire, was mired by constant sectarian conflicts—wars, large and small, that would pit Sunni against Shia, so-called Traditionalist against Rationalist, and a faction led by one family member against that led by another, all vying for power in the center of a dangerous, volatile, and unmanageable region.

Historians suggest that the move of the caliphate from Syria to Mesopotamia was a profound strategic error on the part of the Abbasids. By moving further inland, their access to the Mediterranean was severely stifled. Like ancient Rome, the new empire was soon split into eastern and western spheres, as the wealth and established networks of communication available to the new caliphs could no longer administer the large swaths of land that theoretically lay at their disposal. In North Africa, several independent states emerged out of the power vacuum, and in the Iberian Peninsula, the Umayyads didn't fall when Damascus did—non-Abbasid Muslim rulers continued their presence in Spain until the Christian *Reconquista* was completed in 1492 at the hands of Isabel and Ferdinand.

Politically, the Abbasid caliphate underscored not only the Muslim

Empire's fragile nature but also a failure to recognize the geopolitical trap that Mesopotamia represented. While on the surface its central location may appear as a logical seat for an empire, Iraq had for too long been an intersection of cultural, religious, and imperial ambition. In addition, the challenge of keeping tabs over the rest of the massive empire was all but impossible. For example, Caliph Ma'mun's plans for succession took three months to travel from the mountains of inner Khorasan, in what is now modern Iran, to Baghdad. To get there, the *barid*, the caliph's own postal authority, had to speed from Iran's far reaches; through the valleys of Rayy, near modern-day Tehran; and across the treacherous, narrow passageways of the imposing Zagros Mountains. Snow caused frequent road closures, and nomadic bandits were always on the prowl.

With perfect weather and at breakneck speed, the barid could travel up to seventy-five miles per day, yet the distances in question cover thousands of miles. The caliph, no matter how apt, could hardly maintain his seat of power in Baghdad with any lasting order, let alone properly administer what was destined from the start to be an ungovernable territorial mass—one teeming with ambitious lords and the next messiahs-in-waiting, all eager for their share of political authority.

There was a silver lining to Iraq's location, however. If the Abbasid caliphate was conceived on dangerous territory, it did manage to give birth to what is now regarded as the Golden Age of Islam. Its very place as an intersection between eastern and western lands made Iraq ideal for an exchange not only of armies but also of ideas, architecture, art, and science. Baghdad had been built as a shining city on a hill, and it soon bustled with discussions over Islamic jurisprudence, Greek philosophy, and the latest medical advances. Its palaces were made decadent, and its scribes were fluent in the Iranian tradition of high culture and administration. Like the walled, Jewish cities of pre-Islamic Iraq, Baghdad was built with an eye toward metaphysical grandeur, and the new Muslim rulers spared no expense in this enterprise.

In building his capital, the second Abbasid caliph, al-Mansur, erected a city practically from scratch along the Tigris. Its Persian name, Baghdad, alludes to its destiny as a "God-given" metropolis.[9] And God-given it must have seemed. Baghdad was fashioned in a uniquely aesthetic, circular shape, built by the best masons from across the empire. It was erected between the years 762 and 765, but it continuously remained a work in progress. New palaces were added with every whim of the now self-aggrandizing commanders of the faithful.

Baghdad sought to deliver the promises of early Islam. It was meant to be an ideal community, with a well thought-out balance of markets, streams, houses of worship, and places of learning. Like a Rome for the Islamic world, its city planning was enviable. It kept butcheries and stables away from markets and maintained a sophisticated canal system allowing for moderate defenses, movement, and fresh water for every resident.

From the start, careful zoning ensured enough large space for commerce, including wide avenues (seventy-eight feet wide), streets (twenty-eight feet wide), and plenty of alleys. Mosques and baths were built according to population density, and empty lots were "turned into orchards or [were] cultivated in order that the inhabitants would not be too crowded. A variety of crops ensured harvests in all seasons."[10]

One red flag in the building process was caught early on. A Byzantine ambassador visiting during Mansur's rule found a problem with hosting several bustling marketplaces inside city walls: "All your secrets will be spread throughout the world without your being able to hide them," he counseled the caliph. "The enemy will enter using business as a pretext. Besides, the merchants will travel about and will be able to talk of your most secret affairs."[11] Thus was born the neighborhood of Karkh, just south of the round, walled city, on the western bank of the Tigris. Karkh, Aramaic for "fortified city," acted as the main, separate market district for the town. Today, Karkh makes up a greater part of west Baghdad and includes several neighborhoods inhabited by followers of different sects.

During the early days of Baghdad, planning for sectarian harmony created unintended, and ultimately deadly, consequences. In zoning parts of the city according to clan affiliation, the Abbasid caliphs sought greater surveillance capabilities over their people. Fashioned to nip at the bud any potential insurrection, clan segregation resulted instead in a hardening of sectarian tensions; the seed had been planted for further civil strife. When division didn't do the trick, vigilante justice was always an option. Clan feuds and religious battles often spilled out onto the streets, where mobs killed their enemies with impunity, hanging them for display on one of Baghdad's several bridges—the city's points of highest traffic.

Baghdad's administration was in large part in the hands of Iranians, who quickly became the largest ethnic group in the caliphate. The Abbasids sought to benefit from Iranian royal protocol, scribes, and social institutions. It was the concept of high culture (*adab*), after all, that was passed down from Iranian to Arab hands, and the Abbasids spared no effort to reach the grandiosity of Sasanian Iran. By then, the Islamic empire was a hereditary, monarchic system only marginally shrouded in religious piety. It was a nation of kingship (*mulk*), and not pious leadership (*imama*), so why not learn from pre-Islamic Iran? Why not learn from the real kings? By the time the caliphate was moved from Baghdad to Samarra in 836, subjects requesting an audience would greet the ruler "with verbal formulas of blessing (*ad'ia*), kissing the ground before him" in a protocol fit for an Iranian shah.[12]

The Abbasids' rise and their attainment of the caliphate in 750 signaled a new trend in Islamic politics. Since the Umayyads had already cemented the tradition of hereditary leadership, the question was not whether the caliphate should be passed down within a family, but rather choosing the correct family to lead. The Abbasids proved that a self-proclaimed Imam could attain power over the caliphate, but soon the divisions turned into a question of which family lines were most appropriate: those of Ali or those of Abbas. As the split became more pronounced, the Abbasids increasingly abandoned revolutionary ideals and began adopting a Sunni religious identity.

The Sunni-Shia conflict, then, emerged from this question of familial succession long before doctrinal differences became clearly defined. Because the Shia, the Party of Ali, did not recognize the right of particular dynasties to rule, they soon created their own institutions of religious law and legitimacy, eventually forming their own branch of the Muslim faith.

The Two Orthodoxies

The Hadith, the sayings of the Prophet as narrated by his Companions, were not compiled to any credible extent until the mid-ninth century. Until that time, the messages had varied through centuries of oral transmission, like a game of telephone. But as Traditionalists began to gain ground, they compiled the most "sound" Hadith they could find, naturally with an eye toward their own political and religious worldview.

The Adherents of the Hadith (*As-habu al-Hadith*) were part of a growing movement that believed the Qur'an and the oral traditions were all that was necessary to interpret the laws of God. These two sources of written and oral law, together termed the Traditions (*Sunna*), had always made up the fledgling orthodoxy of Sunni Islam.

The Sunni ulama, the rising clerical class of the Muslim empire, needed to overcome a series of threats, two of which were the veneration of Imams, embodied in Shia doctrine, and the emergence of the Rationalists (*As-habu al-ra'y*, or "Adherents of Reason"), a countervailing school of theology that counseled logical reasoning in the interpretation of Islamic law. This last group, which is often called by the name of one of its factions, the Mu'tazilites, took Iraqi society by storm during the ninth century, fueled by the Arabic translations of Greek philosophy.

The juridical battles were often fought on the streets of Baghdad, with Traditionalists and Rationalists engaging in open civil conflict, most violently during times of transition between one caliph and the next. Caliph Ma'mun, himself a Rationalist, most famously undertook an inquisition against Traditionalist thinkers, during which Traditionalists were subjected to imprisonment and torture if they failed to proclaim the Qur'an as a "created" product (meaning that it hadn't always existed). Calpih al-Mutawakkil finally put an end to the inquisition in 848 and embraced the Traditionalist approach. This helped paved the way for Traditionalism's dominance in Sunni Islam, a trend that continues to this day.

During this formative period, the process of ijtihad, or personal interpretation of law, was alive and well within both Traditionalist and Rationalist schools. Individual clerics would take a position on a given legal question by issuing a *fatwa*, or edict. These fatwas would then be argued between competing clerics until legal consensus was reached.

Via their arguments, individual clerics gained a following and this in turn gave rise to different schools of Sunni Islamic thought. During the ninth century these schools numbered well into the hundreds.[13] Ultimately, however, Sunni believers settled on four main ones—Hanafi, Shafi, Maliki, and Hanbali—, all of which are now considered Traditionalist.

Of these schools, the Hanbali is considered the most conservative, and it was Ahmad ibn Hanbal, its charismatic, ascetic founder, who was famously imprisoned under Ma'mun for refusing to accept the notion of a created Qur'an. Hanbal's school of thought was based on some of the same principles that Sahl, the early ninth-century activist, had embraced during the crisis of succession in Baghdad. Basically, the Hanbali school was a pronounced rejection of Rationalism, and with that it counseled a strict devotion to a literal interpretation of the Qur'an and the Hadith, as it was being assembled at the time. Ibn Hanbal's writings would form the theological backbone of some of the most fundamentalist Islamic thinkers throughout history, from the anti-Crusading Ibn Taymiyya of the late thirteenth century, to Osama bin Laden in the modern day.

As Sunnis settled on the four schools, they largely abandoned ijtihad. Ijtihad had served its purpose as an avenue for different clerics to express individual positions on given issues, but by the tenth century the clerical powers that be, who enjoyed increasing benefits from the state in the form of land grants and other income, agreed that the most important legal questions had already been answered. From the tenth century on, the doors to ijtihad were said to have been closed in Sunni Islam.

Shiism, in contrast, largely appropriated much of the Sunni Rationalist camp's approach to legal reasoning, embracing philosophical inquiry and deductive reasoning, including ijtihad. Just as important, much of the Shia process of codification took place outside of Baghdad, in places like Hilla and the Iranian city of Qom, a trend that only increased the countercultural aspects of Shia theology.

The Shia developed their orthodoxy over an extended period, from the middle of the ninth century until well into the thirteenth. But the biggest push for the codification of law came with the end of the Office of the Imam in the tenth century. During the Imams' lifetimes, a believer could simply look to a living leader for religious guidance, so there was little need for the Shia communities to draw up complicated legal codes. This all changed in 873, when al-Askari, the eleventh Imam, is believed to have died childless at the age of twenty-eight. Shias soon found that Imam al-Askari had actually left a child, Muhammad al-Mahdi, whom he had purposely hidden from the caliph's wrath. In a period known as the Lesser Occultation, a series of intermediaries passed messages between the various communities of believers and Samarra, where the twelfth Imam was believed to be in hiding.

In 941 the intermediaries ceased to be used, at which point al-Mahdi is said to have disappeared for an indefinite time, a period now known as the Great Occultation. With the disappearance of the Imam al-Mahdi, hope for the continuation of the orthodox Shia movement could no longer be found in the words of infallible, living Imams. So, the Twelver, or Itha'ashari, branch of Shiism began to look for ways to codify the Imams' teachings in their absence. Vali Nasr writes, "Just as the dislocating experience of the Babylonian captivity spurred the Israelites to gather together the writings that became the Hebrew Bible, so the imam's occultation convinced the Shia that it was time to set about systematically codifying and organizing their body of religious knowledge."[14]

Thinkers like Muhammad Yaqub al-Kulayni of Qom and Baghdad and Allama al-Hilli of Hilla helped pave the way for the establishment of a Twelver Shia orthodoxy, in which the clergy would carry the spirit of charismatic authority, as it had been embodied in Ali and his descendants from the beginning. After all, through the belief in Ali the earliest followers of the sect had found an avenue to experience that precious time during which the Prophet Muhammad had walked on Earth. By embracing the line of Ali and Fatima, and thus the House of Muhammad, the Shia were longing to recreate this spirit of companionship with the Prophet. "Was it our fault that we were not born at that time?" asked Nasir Khosro, the Persian Shia mystic. "Why should we be deprived of personal contact with the Prophet, thus being (unjustly) punished?"[15] That longing for the Prophet's companionship lies at the core of Shiism.

Al-Kulayni helped put in writing the Imams' sayings, which would serve as a collection to rival the Sunni Hadith. This paved the way for the system called *Usuli*, or "roots-based" jurisprudence. This new movement provided the guidelines for Twelver orthodoxy, with its greatest contribution to modern Shiism being the positioning of the clergy at the top of the pecking order. Because the Imam could no longer be seen or heard, new sources of charismatic authority were needed to placate the Shia community's demands for living religious leadership, and the clergy were willing to oblige.

Another critical development of Shiism came much later, in the thirteenth century, with the official sanctioning of ijtihad, which gave qualified clerics the power to interpret laws in a contemporary context. This de facto power of legislation is practiced today mostly by Shia scholars, and it is a source of continued ideological dispute between the two branches of Islam.

Ijtihad, which comes from the three-letter Arabic root *j-h-d*, is closely related to the word jihad, meaning "struggle." In the case of ijtihad, which means "the state of having exerted oneself," the struggle is an internal one—for knowledge, correct interpretation, and upstanding virtue. Allama al-Hilli, the first cleric to carry the title of ayatollah, defined the process as "the utmost exertion of the faculties to speculate on those questions of the law which are subject to conjecture."[16] Through the process of ijtihad a cleric was able to employ deductive reasoning (a nod to the earlier Sunni and Shia Rationalists of Baghdad) to arrive at a conclusion about how to interpret Islamic law.

This process of arriving at a rational interpretation is based on the assumption of a correlation between religion and reason. This "Rule of Correlation" (*qaidat al-mulazama*) states, "Whatever is ordered by reason, is also ordered by religion."[17] By extension, then, religious rules may be arrived at through the process of applying rational thought. There are, of course, more complicated elements to arriving at judicially sound positions, and the person doing the reasoning has to be considered highly

qualified by his peers and followers. Yet the basics of ijtihad, as it is practiced in Shiism, revolve around a simple concept that attributes a profound rationality to God, a rationality that can be understood in some
way by human kind.

At the heart of ijtihad in Shiism is the idea that every believer is
expected to follow a highly qualified cleric. The cleric, bearing the title
marjatu al-taqlid, can make personal interpretations about a whole host
of issues related to the practice of Islam. What gives particular power
to those who practice ijtihad is the emphasis on following a living cleric,
thus creating a religious or political base for high-ranking individuals.

By the tenth century, the Shia community was coming into its own.
In 963, under the protection of the Buyids, a Shia Iranian dynasty that
briefly ruled over Sunni lands, Baghdad witnessed some of its first public
observations of Husayn's martyrdom on Ashoura. Markets were closed,
"the butchers did not slaughter and the cooks did not cook. People kept
asking for a sip of water" recreating the thirst Husayn and his cohorts
expressed after the caliph's troops cut off access to the Euphrates. In the
markets, tents "were erected and draped with felt covers; women went
round with loose hair to strike their faces . . . lamentations for the death
of al-Husayn sprang up."[18]

Parallel communities of the faithful, one Shia, one Sunni, began to
settle in place with their powerful rituals, clerical classes, and fervent
students. There were still internal differences within the sects. Twelver
Shia fought Ismaili Shia, and Hanafi Sunnis took on their Shafi brethren.
But Islam as a worldview was becoming clearly divided between those
who accepted the succession of the Prophet as it occurred and those who
recognized the infallible nature of Ali and the Office of the Imam. This
basic disagreement served as the intellectual dividing line of the Sunni-
Shia conflict we see today.

5

A REGION DIVIDED

The Sunni-Shia divisions of medieval Islam increased in a region that lacked a single central Islamic government. Because Islam was understood and accepted as the one true faith by the vast majority of people in the Middle East, religious debates pivoted on the question of what Islam actually was. Needless to say, this opened rancorous avenues for debate and bloodshed over who was right and who was wrong in his interpretation. Those who sought to rule empires were claiming to be leaders of a caliphate, so it was impossible to separate religious leadership from temporal rule: to be a political leader, one had to claim some level of divinity, or at the very least extreme piety. To be an emperor, one had to call himself a Commander of the Faithful.

While divisions occurred on the ground within any given community and at any given time, the region at large was often at war with itself, polarized into two camps—one in the east, usually based in Iran, and one in the west, seated in Egypt or Anatolia. This dynamic tore the region apart, and those caught in the middle of changing governments often found themselves under sudden persecution and attack.

Not unlike the Soviets and Americans during the Cold War, eastern and western empires made use of orchestrated propaganda campaigns to paint their enemies as unholy. While the Cold War parties used terms such as "imperialist" or "communist" to attack the enemy within, Muslim minorities were often marginalized as extremists or worse yet, heretics.

This east-west divide had been at play long before the advent of Islam, when Zoroastrian Iran was fighting Christian Rome. But after Islam, particularly starting in the tenth century, the divisions were colored mostly in terms of Sunni against Shia. Of course, the terms "Sunni" and "Shia" obscure a larger splintering of belief (Islam was never merely bipolar), but because the strongholds of east and west were continuously the most assertive, they found that adopting a version of one of these two branches would be useful as a tool for consolidating power internally, and thus they could more easily identify friends and detractors. In turn, these imperial policies helped cement orthodox versions of the two sects, since every ruler had to explicitly communicate what he meant by "Islam," and why his version of it was superior to all others.

During this period the Islamic community in the Middle East began splitting into these polarized camps, while smaller vassal states found it increasingly convenient to pick sides or merely play one empire against another. That the leaders in question practiced *Realpolitik* does not mean that honest religion convictions were a minor consideration. In fact, religion was the tool that kept the rulers' legitimacy alive and, in good times, the majority of their subjects from rising up in mutiny.

One important note should be added. To speak of "eastern" and "western" poles does not mean attributing a kind of free will or agency to geographic locations. Rather, it is in these geographic centers that rising dynasties were able to secure their base of support, and ultimately their empires. More often than not, this had to do with the existence of an established administrative class in these areas, some of which hailed back to Roman and Sasanian times.

Since existing empires were often unable to control the political and religious behavior of their subjects, believers could choose between the various sects to follow, in a kind of market of belief. It shouldn't be surprising, then, that the sects which often became dominant within particular communities were those that stood in opposition to the religious propaganda of the established empire. That is, to revolt against your ruler would often (though not always) mean adopting a different religion.

The Fatimids and the Seljuks

As the region was splitting up in the tenth century, Shiism achieved a feat it had not experienced since Ali's caliphate three hundred years before. A powerful Shia country, which also happened to be Arab, was established. The Fatimids were an Ismaili Shia dynasty, meaning they belonged to a branch of Shiism that had split from what is now the majority, Twelver branch. The division happened when the Ismailis rejected the ascension of Musa al-Kadhim (father of Reza) to the Imamate following the death of the fifth Shia Imam, Jafar al-Sadiq, in 765. The Ismailis believed that Jafar's son Ismail had not died before his father had, as the Twelvers contended, and thus Ismail was the rightful Imam and that his bloodline, and not that of Musa, should have been followed.

The Fatimids undertook a military campaign in North Africa and Sicily starting in 909, and by 969 they had captured Egypt and built up Cairo to serve as the capital of their growing empire. The first Fatimid caliph, Abdullah al-Mahdi, was a living Ismaili Imam, and in the eyes of his followers, his rule represented the rightful succession of the Imamate.

At their peak of power, the Fatimids mastered the use of ideological mobilization. Weekly lectures were written and disseminated across their domains to keep the faithful up to the date on the expected communal roles of the caliph, his court, and the people. More ambitious, they sent out missionaries across the vast expanses of the Muslim world to preach the Ismaili faith and the Fatimids' political goodwill. The missionaries, who viewed Cairo as a kind of shining city on a hill, risked life, limb, and pride to travel throughout hostile territories to spread their message. Through their dawa, the Fatimids were able to upstage the Abbasid Empire, a power that was now mostly symbolic, given the rise of Iranian and Turkic overlords in Iran and Iraq. At their height, the Fatimids controlled "Egypt, Syria, North Africa, Sicily, the Red Sea coast of Africa, the Yemen and the Hijaz in Arabia, with the holy cities of Mecca and Medina."[1]

As would often be the case in the Middle East, the Fatimids were a minority in their own lands. This is because fighting on behalf of the

Fatimids did not necessarily correlate with embracing Ismaili ideology, it simply meant upholding Fatimid political rule. And while the empire "demanded of every citizen an oath of allegiance to the ruler,"[2] the dynasty is remembered for its respect of Sunnis and members of other confessions.

Back in the Abbasid domains, a massive incursion of foreign fighters had weakened the caliphate's eastern lands so that by the late tenth century ethnic Iranians had established the Shia Buyid dynasty through much of Mesopotamia, and by 975 ethnic Turks, who had flooded the region via the mountains of Khorasan, set up a powerful Sunni state under the Ghaznavids in Iran and Central Asia. The official nail on the Abbasids' coffin finally came with the entrance of the Seljuks into the region.

In 1035 this nomadic Oghuz-Turkish tribe came in from the vast and wild Central Asian steppes, across the Oxus River, and into inner Khorasan,[3] from which they marched into Baghdad and established their leader, Toghril, as sultan. Through their entrance into the region, the Seljuks changed the face and ethnic makeup of the Middle East forever. First, they led a period known as the Sunni revival and with it what became the temporary elimination of Shia empires from the region. Second, the Seljuks placed the caliphate in ethnic Turkish hands, a trend that continued until the office was abolished in 1924.

Traveling Sufi mystics in Central Asia had converted the Seljuks, who had taken their name from their eponymous leader, Seljuk, to Islam. Sufism, which exists within both Sunni and Shia Islam, stresses the emotional connection—the oneness—between mankind and God. Unlike the more orthodox strands of Sunni or Shia Islam, Sufism places less focus on scriptural study and more on the love and affection between believer and deity, to some degree comparable to Chasidic ideas in Judaism.

Some of the greatest poets of the Islamic world, mystics like Hafez and Rumi, can be tied to strong Sufi ideals, and to this day some Sufis, particularly in Turkey and the Kurdish region of Iran, practice their religion by reaching a state of hypnotic trance, usually by way of a repetitive action such as spinning, praying aloud, or singing. Today's Whirling Dervishes, who twirl for hours on end in prayer in their red fez caps, are perhaps the most internationally recognized of all Sufi orders.

Because early Islamic conversion drives from the Arab world into the Turkish-speaking Central Asian steppes were usually carried out by wondering travelers and not organized state-driven campaigns, Turkic peoples soon became associated with various strands of Sufism. The farther north and northeast one traveled from the epicenter of orthodox study in Mesopotamia and Arabia, the more likely one was to encounter a traveling Sufi wise man.

Given the overlap between Ismaili Shiism and Sufism at the time, particularly with regard to the veneration of living leaders, one would have expected the Fatimids and the Seljuk Sufis to be compatible on some level. But they weren't. The Seljuks' newfound geopolitical position in the heart of Iran and Mesopotamia (and the coming expansion west to Anatolia itself) made the Fatimids their biggest obstacle for regional domination. The Fatimids became the Seljuks' mortal enemies.

On taking power in Iran and Iraq, the Seljuks jettisoned their personal Sufi identity in favor of a much more stringent, literalist approach to religion. After all, the Fatimids had cornered the market of free-spirited diversity. The Seljuks had to counter with hardened orthodoxy. This imperial competition, and not personal preference, led the Seljuks into strict Sunnism and into a fight of their lives against the Shia "heretics." It was not enough to belong to a different political order. The Seljuks had to offer an alternative worldview: a more correct interpretation and expression of the Muslim faith.

Notwithstanding official Seljuk ideology, Shiism did not fade away in eastern lands and Twelver Shias did not experience the same fate as Ismailis. In fact, during the Seljuk period Iranians adopted Shiism in greater numbers, and even Sunni Iranians were known to take part in the rituals of Ashoura, which included weeping for the fallen Husayn and actually cursing the names of the first three caliphs—Abu Bakr, Umar, and Uthman.[4] Despite the orthodox movements of the ninth and tenth centuries, Islam was still malleable and regionally diverse as late as the eleventh century.

As the Seljuks gained strength and Fatimid power diminished, large numbers of Ismailis are thought to have converted to Twelver Shiism, if only in hopes of evading persecution. From the turn of the eleventh century on, large Twelver communities sprang up in Bahrain and Jabal Amil (the hilly region of south Lebanon), many converting from the Ismaili branch.[5] These communities later played a pivotal role in the revival of Shiism as a powerful contender for the hearts and minds of people in the region. For now, however, the Sunni revival was still in effect.

A vigorous effort to codify Sunni law, spread its teachings, and cement its appeal among the people followed the Fatimids' demise. In this effort, the Seljuks built the first *madrasa* in Baghdad. While this Arabic word is the generic term for "school," here it refers to a center of religious study, an Islamic seminary fashioned after the Shia centers of learning in Mesopotamia (which themselves were likely inspired by the Jewish seminaries, or *batei midrash*). The Seljuks spread this Sunni madrasa system throughout their empire, not only to undo the legacy of Ismaili missions, but to suppress theological divisions between the disparate Sunni factions. Students of the madrasa learned the Qur'an and the oral traditions of the Prophet, as well as the dominant trends in Sunni Islamic interpretation, which came primarily from the Hanafite branch of Sunnism.[6]

By 1169, the anti-Crusading commander Nur al-Din captured Egypt and undertook a campaign to fight European Christians and concurrently suppress all remnants of Shiism. His successor, the legendary Kurdish sultan Salah al-Din (known in the West as Saladin), officially abolished the Fatimid state in North Africa in 1172. Through the Sunni revival, large-scale Shia rule in the Middle East was over, at least for the moment being.

The Mamluks and the Mongols

Despite the religious triumph of Sunnism, the Middle East continued to be divided into spheres of power, and before long the Seljuks themselves suffered a devastating loss in the east to hordes of invading Mongols—the successors of Genghis Khan's drive for conquest, which had begun in East and Central Asia.

The Middle East was soon split between the Egyptian Sunni state that Saladin had helped create in the west and the new Mongol state founded in the east. Though both were Sunni in character (the regional Mongol leader, or *il-khan*, converted to Islam in 1295), they were diametrically opposed in their quest for supremacy. Just as important, both faced an underground, secret movement of Shia opposition—radical Ismailis ready to kill without notice and be martyred in the process—and both, to varying degrees, had to cope with encroaching European Crusaders. This rise of the Mongol Empire, or Il-Khanate, and the concurrent cloak-and-dagger operations by the Ismailis began a trend of deadly espionage, murder, and duplicity that to this day characterizes the region's feared and despised intelligence services.

Reuven Amitai of Hebrew University has written extensively on the geopolitical dynamics during this period. In his book *Mongols and Mamluks*, he provides an overview of the hot and cold wars that raged between the two polar opposites. He explains that the fast-paced Mongol conquest that ravaged the Middle East was in part owing to the fact that "territorial expansion into neighboring areas was a *sine qua non* of nomadic states in the Eurasian steppes, motivated as they were by the desire to control the manufactured and agricultural goods which could only be found there."[7]

Once the Mongols entered Iran via Khorasan, they overran much of the region, eventually taking the seat of the now merely titular caliphate in Baghdad in 1258. The extent of Mongol destruction is debated, but to the people of the region, particularly those in Iran, it is remembered in lore as something of an Armageddon. Needless to say, much of the sour tone toward the Mongols stems from the fact that until 1295 the Mongols were long-haired shamanists, foreigners with a blatantly pagan way of life.

On the other side of the region were the Mamluks, a group of military slaves leftover from Saladin's campaigns, who came to usurp power for themselves in Egypt in 1250 with a *coup d'état*. The Mamluks were a caste of Central Asian Turkish origin, the members of whom were gathered from their homes at a young age, taught the ways of Islam, and brought up to be fighters beholden to the rulers who employed them across the Muslim world. As it often turns out, these praetorian guards offered both a convenience and a threat to those who depended on them for protection. Certainly, they did not have allegiances to speak of inside the Middle East, but they did come to share a powerful loyalty to one another.

When the Mamluk state was formed in Egypt, it stood as the single greatest obstacle to Mongol advances. The Mamluks had been the center of resistance to the European Crusades, and they sought Sunni unity by adopting "the principle of the equality of the four Sunnite schools of law" as a matter of policy.[8] As the Mongols had stripped Seljuk power in the east, the Mamluks had taken up the banner of anti-Crusading efforts.

When the Mongols attempted to crush the Mamluks with a joint Mongol-European attack on Egypt, Europe, perhaps fearing the power of an unchecked Mongol hegemon in the region, repeatedly failed to reciprocate the Il-Khanate's diplomatic advances. In fact, in the Syrian Levant French troops stood aside and let the Mamluks take the fight to a limited, forward-operating Mongol force in 1260, an event that became a lifeline for the anti-Crusading Mamluks. That same year Mamluk general Baybars defeated the Mongol forces in the famous Battle of Ayn Jalut (now in the West Bank). Baybars was known to be anti-Mongol through and through, and legend remembers him "having both verbally rebuked and physically beaten . . . the main proponent of submission" to the Mongols.[9]

A cold war took hold between the two camps, with skirmishes erupting along the border of the two empires. Baybars, an effective and powerful ruler who was confronted with the dual menace of French Crusaders in the Levant and the Mongol empire based in Iran, made use of an extensive spy network, whose operatives established contacts with Muslim lords across the region, served as an early warning system for Mongol movements, and helped incite disturbances within Mongol domains.

But Baybars' spies were more than mere intelligence gatherers. Amitai recounts the story of a forged letter of "gratitude" sent to a group of Baghdad-based Armenian Catholics, who had been staunch allies of the Mongols. This letter was meant to suggest that the Christians were providing intelligence to the Mamluks, and Baybars arranged for the purposeful interception of this letter, which would surely end up in the Mongol ruler's hands. The letter had its intended result, and the Catholics were summarily executed.

Baybars had more tricks up his sleeve, and he was not beyond employing a radical sect of Ismaili Shiism for his own devices. Leftover from the dissolution of the Fatimid Empire, the Nizaris were unique in their extreme positions, secrecy, and willingness to kill large numbers of those they considered heretics. This group, which brought fear to the hearts of Muslim and Christian alike, would later give rise to the term "assassin," the Europeanized inflection of *hashashin* (an epithet to insinuate the group was prone to taking hashish).

The Nizaris operated from independent castle-states scattered across the Iranian and Syrian landscape. From their fortresses, they would dispatch operatives far and wide, some charged with promoting their dawa, others as covert agents to set up sleeper cells that would blend in with the target populations, sometimes going unrecognized for years at a time. Nizaris were known to befriend their victims, often gaining employment as government officials and remaining unsuspected until they suddenly struck, usually with a dagger, and usually as a response to some policy of persecution against their coreligionists.

The Nizaris, or *fidayeen* (those who seek martyrdom), as they called themselves, can be thought of as some of the first practitioners of suicide terrorism in the Middle East, since they were not expected to survive their spectacular missions, and instilling fear was certainly part of the Nizari agenda. David C. Rapoport writes: "Since orthodox Muslims understood the importance of internal support, the Assassins manipulated apprehensions by implicating enemies as accomplices—a maneuver that multiplied suspicions and confusion."[10]

During the periods of Nizari terror, Sunni Islam began to entrench its orthodox, anti-Shia positions, in part led by influential figures like Ibn Taymiyya, the Mamluk's *Shaykh al-Islam* (highest cleric), who actively persecuted Shias within his domains and came to represent the kind of puritanism that would inspire the likes of Osama bin Laden centuries later. This concept of state persecution is important to note, since prior to the sixteenth century Muslims would often combine Sunni and Shia convictions, particularly in mixed societies like Iran. A Shia might venerate the first three caliphs, while a Sunni might heap praise on the Twelve Imams. Such intersectarian theology could hardly be imagined today, when most Shias do not think highly of the first three caliphs, while some conservative Sunnis may view the veneration of the Imams as idolatry. This hardening of Sunni-Shia identities only increased over time as the power of particular states became stronger, and the need to pursue an official propaganda meant demonizing competing branches of the faith.

Away from power, Twelver Shias turned inward during this period of Mongol-Mamluk bipolarity, and worked to further develop the tenets of their sect. The most significant strides in creating a lasting Twelver Shia community of scholars were made in Iraq, as well as in Jabal Amil and the Beqa Valley (modern-day Lebanon).[11] In fact, it was from Lebanon that the new Iranian dynasty, the Safavids, drew its recruits to usher in the massive conversion of Iran into Shiism and forever change the face of the Middle East.

The Ottomans and the Safavids

The Ottoman Empire emerged after centuries of Turkic migration from the Central Asian steppes. The gradual trickle initially took the form of tactical incursions by nomadic tribes seeking loot. But starting in 1256, when the Mongols turned Muslim lands upside down in a campaign of conquest, the doors to Central Asian migration swung wide open.

The Ottomans, like the Seljuks, took their name from their leader, in their case Osman (the Turkish rendering of the name Uthman). As such, they were strict Sunnis in matters of state; though, consistent with the way in which many Central Asians had come to the faith, Sufi mysticism had been their original calling.

Starting in the fourteenth century, the Ottomans made incursions into southeastern Europe, leaving behind a Muslim legacy that is still shared by populations in Albania, Bosnia-Herzegovina, and Kosovo. In 1453 the Ottomans went on to take Constantinople, where Mehmed II proclaimed himself Caesar of the Roman Empire (*Kaysar-i Rum*).

With Christianity declining fast in the eastern Mediterranean, such was the panic in central and western Europe that the papacy tried to muster all the European unity it could find (and even reached out to smaller, rival Muslim Anatolian kingdoms for help). Soon enough, polarization took hold between the continent of Europe and the Middle East, proving that the process that hardens sectarian animosity knows no cultural or geographic bounds.

Tomas Mastnak reminds us that the communal concept of "Europa" did not implicitly exist in the identity of the continent's inhabitants. Rather, Mediterranean-based identities, for example, crisscrossed the European, African, and Asian continents seamlessly, making a Sicilian culturally closer to a North African than to a German. Europe as a community was in large part formed by the European Crusades and, just as important, by the Ottoman conquest of Constantinople and the Christian response to it. Long before Edmund Burke famously proclaimed, "No citizen of Europe could be altogether an exile in any part of it,"[12] Europe had to learn to see itself as a singular entity, and that is exactly what the Ottoman advances inspired. Mastnak writes, "Formative of Christendom, that fundamentally inimical attitude toward the Muslims, had not only survived the disintegration of Christendom as the medieval form of Western unity but also lent its creative potential to the formation of the new Western unity: Europe."[13]

The Ottoman Empire's legacy of polarization was not restricted to Europe. The east again made a comeback, with Iran offering an equal and opposite reaction to Ottoman strength. As had been the case during the Seljuks' reign, a Turkish family rose to orchestrate a challenge from the east, one that would reenergize the region and bring a cultural, military, and political revival to the Iranian plateau.

A Sufi sect loosely ascribing to the Shafi school of Sunni Islam, the Safavids were a family of Tajik origin, meaning they were Persian-speaking Turks. Like the Ottomans, the Safavids owed their lineage to a particular leader, a charismatic individual who had fashioned a religious (and consequently political) movement of spiritual renewal. Their leader was a mystic named Safi al-Din (1252–1334), who hailed from Ardabil, in what is now northwestern Iran, along the Caspian Sea. Having ascended to influence during the era of Mongol rule over Iran, Safi was a holy man with a network of disciples that reached far and wide, from Central Asia all the way to Egypt.

Needless to say, such spiritual fealty came with political power, and local rulers were conscious to treat Safi with due deference, all while his disciples saw him as something of a divine figure—one of a large number of living saints that hailed from Iran and Central Asia. Free-spirited in typical Sufi fashion, Safi is said to have preached "a renewal of Islam which would transcend the dogmatism of the theologians and the squabbling of the heretics."[14] It is ironic that Safi embraced the kind of liberalism, which the powerful dynasty bearing his name would later seek to stamp out.

Over the next two centuries, the Safavid order became increasingly militarized, taking in Turkomen nomadic soldiers hailing from the dominant White Sheep and Black Sheep tribal confederations that ruled Iran and Azerbaijan following the decline of Mongol power. Marching with his troops of believers, a militant order known as the *Qizilbash* ("Red Heads," after the color of their hats), Safavid leader Ismail I conquered Tabriz in 1501 and founded the Safavid Empire in Iran.

Ismail's success rested in large part on his ability to calm controversies of faith, and his Sufi background was balanced with a state policy of forced conversion to Shiism, a practice he adopted to counter the Ottoman Sunnis. By strategically creating a home for Shias from around the region, Ismail was able to pick up the slack that floundering Fatimids had left behind and that no other Shia dynasty had been far reaching enough to take up. That Ismail was himself a Sufi and self-proclaimed messiah was beside the point—the Middle East, like everywhere else in the world, is a place where a ruler's politics has always trumped religious considerations.

Like the Ottomans, the Safavids soon adopted orthodoxy as a practical matter. They deescalated the messianic rhetoric of the extremists, or ghulat, within their court, particularly those clerics preaching the expected return of the Imam. Instead the Safavids opted for a more cautious and conservative approach, officially teaching that the Hidden Imam was a figure of Biblical proportions, one who, like Abraham and Noah, could simply outlive the rest of us.[15] Safavid subjects were from then on implored not to expect a hasty return of the messiah and instead were invited to join in the empire's consolidation of power and stability, their kingdom on earth.

On the patriotic front, the new dynasty embraced a much more Iranian identity, resurrecting the Persian New Year, or *Nowrooz*, at the royal court. The widespread and mainstream embrace of this pagan ritual in Iran continues to the present day, even in the Islamic Republic, where being Iranian continues to be just as important, if not more important, than being Muslim.

As the empire grew, orthodoxy was further applied. The conservative, clergy-centered Twelver branch of Shiism had already left its mark on Lebanon's Jabal Amil and the holy cities of Iraq, but it took the Safavids to bring it to Iran in full force. Starting around 1533, a prayer leader was appointed "in every village to instruct the people in the tenets of Twelver Shi'ism."[16] Iran was now a Shia state.

Needless to say, those on the receiving end of this fast-paced, mass conversion to Shiism were the Sunni citizens, as well as less stringent followers of Islam. Toward the end of the sixteenth century, Shah Tahmasp moved his capital to Qazvin, where he closed down taverns and brothels and placed the city under "increased surveillance by his propagandizing agents."[17] (The shah must have failed in "purifying" the city because to this day Qazvin is the butt of countless Iranian jokes as a place of ill repute.)

Sunnis who refused to convert were driven out or summarily executed, and under Tahmasp the name Ali was added to the official call to prayer in every city and hamlet, even over the objections of a Shia clergy that did not consider this order to be religiously necessary or even appropriate. What mattered to the Safavids, however, was not religious purity but the assertion of power. In this sense, the name Ali was merely a synonym for Safavid rule, and thus it had to be heard and heeded across the land.

On the international front, Safavid Iran enjoyed a modicum of European support in its fight against Anatolia, while its Ottoman rivals coordinated geopolitical strategy with Central Asian Uzbegs—Sunnis who dwelled in large numbers in the always restless region of Khorasan. Throughout the much of the sixteenth century, however, the Ottomans had the upper hand. Initially, they were able to simultaneously stave off Iranian growth while fighting leftover Mamluks in Egypt and pushing their way through the eastern Mediterranean and into Europe. Not since the early days of the caliphate had a Muslim empire achieved so much so fast. In 1514, not fourteen years after the Safavids' rise, the Ottomans took the Iranian capital of Tabriz and temporarily occupied it. Achieving superpower status, the Ottomans defeated the Spanish Armada at Djerba (1560), off the coast of Tunisia. Christian Europe's anxiety did not subside until the Holy League defeated the Ottoman navy at the historic Battle of Lepanto in 1571.

Throughout this period, a series of Safavid-Ottoman wars rocked the region, often due to Iran's insistence on controlling Baghdad and the Shia holy cities of southern Iraq. It was during the reign of Iranian shah Abbas I in the early 1600s (and with the advice of the adventurous, traveling English brothers Sir Anthony and Sir Robert Shirley) that the Safavids reorganized their military along European lines and began having more luck wresting Iraqi lands from the Ottomans. Between 1508 and 1638, Baghdad changed hands four times between the Ottomans and Safavids.

With military power came the ability to control expressions of faith, and periods of Ottoman and Safavid bipolarity coincide with the meticulous control of both Sunni and Shia orthodoxies. In Ottoman lands, clerics teaching at a madrasa or working at courts across the Turkish-speaking parts of the empire "were ranked, graded and pensioned under central state auspieces."[18] Muslim judges were sent far and wide throughout the empire to be the sultan's eyes and ears, reporting on the conduct (and misconduct) of merchants and administrators. Once the domain of revolution, the clergy of the Ottoman Empire became inexorably tied to the state.

From a strategic perspective, the Ottomans' numerous wars with Europe had left them blockaded at sea by the navies of Spain and Portugal, which were acting on the papacy's behest. Their access, then, to the holy cities of the Hijaz in Arabia, as well as to the trade routes that led east, was severely hampered from all sides. Just as alarming, Shia political ideology was permeating the Ottoman state, raising fears of a Safavid-supported fifth column in Anatolia and Syria.[19]

To be sure, Iran's relationship with Jabal Amil was the sine qua non of Safavid strategy against Ottoman Turkey. While many Lebanese clerics descended on Iran to help in the massive conversion to Twelver Shiism, Iran's growing influence helped steer some Ismaili believers in Jabal Amil, leftover from Fatimid times, toward a conversion to the rising Twelver ideology. The special relationship between the Shia clerical communities of Iran and those in Lebanon was only beginning to take hold, but to this day continues to grow in meaning and importance.

Modern Divisions: The Arab States and Iran

The Ottoman Empire began to decline after the large-scale incursion of Europe into the Middle East, and the ensuing power vacuum left openings for new social and political movements, most of which were nudged along by European foreign ministries that in the early twentieth century were already thirsting for oil and longing for the dissolution of the Turkish Empire.

At that time, such countries as Egypt, Syria, Jordan, and Turkey itself, were overrun with popular movements of independence and reform. At times, these societies grasped at straws when constructing a national identity, but their efforts were eventually boosted by a good-hearted promise made by U.S. president Woodrow Wilson, champion of the concept of self-determination, that their sovereignty as a people would be recognized following the First World War.

One family that embraced the new world order was the House of Saud, which had been an erstwhile opponent to Ottoman colonialism and had been fighting for centuries to command the entire Arabian Peninsula. The family, led by Muhammad bin Saud, had entered an alliance with the House of Shaykh in 1744, forming a marriage of convenience that has lasted to this day. The House of Shaykh was led by Muhammad ibn Abd al-Wahhab and his fellow clanspeople, who became famous for their ultraorthodox ways, as well as their prowess on the field of battle.

For the Wahhabis, the mission of armed struggle was directed not only at Ottoman colonialists but also at the Shia, whom they saw as apostates (*kafir*)—the worst kind of heretics. Yet his anti-Shia campaign resulted in one of the most ironic of all developments in the history of the Sunni-Shia conflict.

While the Wahhabis were instrumental in helping the House of Saud consolidate its power over the peninsula and eventually contributed to the defeat the rival House of Rashid in Arabia, their most significant fingerprint on the Middle Eastern landscape comes from their unwitting propagation of Shiism in Iraq, largely as a result of a general revulsion that Wahhabi tactics inspired in the country. When Wahhabi bands started making incursions into southern Iraq in the early 1800s, Iraqi Sunni tribes were caught off-guard by the brutality and impunity with which the Wahhabis attacked and pillaged their countryside.

The largely nomadic Sunnis, who were of Arabian origin themselves and belonged to tribes that had migrated out of the Arabian Peninsula over the course of centuries, had much in common with the Wahhabi attackers, and they had little reason to become Shia themselves. At the time, the urban centers of southern Iraq were still predominantly Shia but were not as densely populated, and even then, they were largely foreign-run and uninhabited. Arabs made up "only a very small fraction of the student population" within the seminaries. Iranian Shias, determined to safeguard the holy cities of their faith, had made significant efforts to maintain the sanctity of the shrines through investment and pilgrimage. And since funds for clerical scholarship were often allocated by national origin and "most of their own countrymen did not channel sufficient resources for their upkeep," Iraqi Arabs tended to get the short end of the stick in these houses of learning.[20]

With the Wahhabis pillaging the region, the Sunni nomads began to look for protection inside the cities, and in a massive effort to fit in with their urban peers, they converted in staggering numbers to the Shia confession. This process was compounded by a policy of settlement the Ottomans had instituted in 1831, forcing large nomadic tribes with roots in Arabia to take up the plow and build permanent dwellings. The ensuing crisis of identity, as well as the need for protection, led to the majority Shia demographics we see in Iraq today.

Politically, the Wahhabi and Shia communities have been butting heads ever since. In 1920 Iraqi Shia revolutionaries mentioned the declaration of jihad against Wahhabis as one of their key planks. And in 1943 Ayatollah Khomeini used a major early work, *Kashf al-Asrar* ('The Revelation of Secrets'), to attack both secularists and Wahhabis, the latter of whom he called "wild and savage attackers of the Shi'a Holy Places of Iraq."[21]

It is tragic that so many of the suicide bombers of post-2003 Iraq, who have detonated their payload in crowded Shia markets and places of worship have been the very Wahhabis whose ideological (and perhaps in some cases, genealogical) ancestors helped turn Iraq into a majority Shia country. Polarization, even confined to a few hundred square miles, can be a powerful instrument of religious conversion and long-lasting political divisions.

Today, regional polarization marches on. Iran continues to stand on one side, and the new states of the Arab Middle East on the other. In recent times, Saudi Arabia has joined fellow Sunni countries Egypt and Jordan in their efforts to curb Iranian influence. But Iran's power has only increased with the establishment of yet another friendly regime in Iraq, one that follows a long line of Mesopotamian-based states that have served as an Iranian buttress against west-based powers.

One may be tempted to view the Islamic Republic of Iran's contention against these states as a result of Sunni-Shia divisions, but particular theologies have been only a tool in the conflict, and not the source of it. Throughout history, Iran and its competitors consistently vacillated between Sunni and Shia rule, usually with the aim of countering whatever the other side's confession was.

The divisions originated in a climate rife with the three catalysts of sectarian conflict. First, there were charismatic leaders, Sunni and Shia alike, each promoting their own versions of the true practice of Islam. These leaders inspired fierce antagonism, but because admission into a group was less about ethnicity than it was about expressed belief, the lines between groups were often blurred and malleable, as an individual could join a sect through simple conversion and the death of a movement could occur on the whim of shifting political winds.

Second, the breakdown of state authority in the region consistently allowed communal figures to rise up and seek a state of their own. This had become the norm in the Middle East, where overarching empires lacked the administrative abilities or military power to cover the expanses of territory they purported to claim. Unlike in post-Roman Europe, where small, defendable, often ethnically based states were the rule and not the exception, the Middle East throughout most of its history was a place where a single family could come to claim over half of the entire region with a coup or a small, localized war. The stakes were high, but the prize was always too difficult to keep and most lands remained either in the care of vassal states or as ungovernable, independent cities hosting the next revolutionary movement-in-waiting.

In present times, this lack of cohesion has reappeared as minority groups continue to govern over a majority population. In Syria, the power is concentrated among members of the Alawite branch of Islam, who nevertheless rule over an overwhelmingly Sunni state, and in Saddam Hussein's Iraq, the minority Arab Sunnis governed over majority Shia Arabs and Sunni Kurds. Preference in high positions of government was then given to members of the western town of Tikrit, from which Saddam and much of his political clique hailed. The opposite of democratic pluralism, the few have always ruled the many in the Middle East. Saudi Arabia today is no different. It is ruled by a single family, supported by a religious class of clerics, many of whom are direct descendants of Abd al-Wahhab's fighters. The Saudi clerics, who are the guardians of the country's ultraconservative religious laws, are most specifically associated with the Qahtani clan of Quraysh tribal origin.

At the end of the day, the region's political actors are always treading on shaky ground, since, save for Iran, Turkey and Israel—countries that have strong, unifying national identities—, the modern Middle East is founded on largely artificial concepts. Saudi is a family, Syria is a region, Iraq is an idea, and Jordan is a river—none of these countries constitutes a "nation" in the more profound sense of the word.

Last, the Sunni-Shia conflict was sparked by a catalyst of geopolitical battles. Starting in the tenth century, the internal fissures at the regional level gave way to the east-west bipolarity that had been at play since late antiquity. Instead of Christian Rome fighting Zoroastrian Iran, the new polarity was fought in terms of Sunni versus Shia, with each region taking turns in its espousal of a given Muslim sect. And with the conscious use of religious propaganda by the state, orthodox versions of the two branches began to take shape, aided by the treasuries of host empires.

At its epicenter, the Sunni-Shia conflict was an Iraqi phenomenon ignited during the first Muslim civil war. The battle was between the Party of Ali and that of the late Uthman over the control of the empire, but it soon took on a life of its own. Though Ali was assassinated, most ardent followers never gave up his claim to leadership, and his son Husayn, the Prophet's grandson, was martyred at Karbala in 680 to become the symbol of a powerful, rising movement. Shiism still came in many forms by the eighth century, and the Abbasid caliphate used its revolutionary rhetoric to attain power and establish Iraq as its political anchor. But with that came only more problems in a land that had been at the crossroads of civilizations and armies from the beginning of history. Baghdad, the newly built center of kingly excess and religious piety, became a bloody battlefield of ideas, sects, and familial rivalries.

The Sunni-Shia conflict in the Middle East, as an expression of the three catalysts, continues to rear its ugly head, with its focal point emerging once again in Iraq. It was all too predictable that Mesopotamia, the battleground that gave birth to the conflict some thirteen centuries ago, blew up again in 2003 with street-level sectarian killings and the proxy support of the ambitious countries that surround it.

6

AN IMAGINED LAND

While the land of Mesopotamia is as old as time, the country we now call Iraq was born only in 1920. It was a construct of British imperialism, and like so many other products of colonial rule, it did not reflect any coherent "nation" or "people."

Iraq was born out of a combination of the Ottoman provinces of Baghdad, Mosul and Basra. The Sunni-favored structure in the region, as set up by Turkish colonialism, was eagerly continued by Great Britain when the European superpower split up Ottoman lands in the course and aftermath of the First World War. The Sykes-Picot Agreement of 1916 gave France Syria and Kurdish Iraq, and Britain the rest of Mesopotamia, as well as Transjordan. Eventually, France gave Kurdish Mosul to Britain, which in turn joined it with Basra and Baghdad to create modern Iraq.

Though both the Ottomans and the British colonized Iraq, their designs for Mesopotamia could not have been more different. The Ottoman presence was part of a larger policy of fortifying Sunni rule in Shia Iran's front yard. Given the importance of the holy Shia cities of southern Iraq, the Iranian ulama continued to play a significant role in the maintenance of religious sites and centers of learning in Mesopotamia long after Iran had lost its grip over the country.

To this day, many of the most prominent Shia clerical families in

Iraq have strong familial and personal connections to Iran. The Ottomans needed to maintain Sunni dominance in Iraq then, not just a matter of religious sensibilities, but owing to a deep-seated fear of Iranian influence over their domains.

For Britain, which landed an expeditionary force in southern Iraq in 1914, control of the country was only of relative strategic importance, and when anti-European resentment boiled over in 1932, the Europeans were all too eager to leave. Even from the beginning of the League of Nations mandate of 1920, which placed Mesopotamia under Britain's "care," the British Foreign Office was aware of its limited ability to control Iraq's affairs in too overt a manner.

The appearance of self-rule thus took precedence over efficient administration in what otherwise could be considered a colony. Because Britain wanted to pay lip service to the narrative of anticolonialism and self-determination but still wanted some control over Iraq's future, its administration of the country quickly degenerated into an exercise that was as hypocritical as it was mediocre. Gone was the brutal efficiency the British crown had employed in India. Postwar Iraq would have to be ruled haphazardly, underhandedly, and ultimately, ineffectively.

When Britain left Iraq in 1932 and especially when it finally left the region for good in 1971, a period of relative Iraqi independence followed. But Iraqi self-reliance came at a cost to its neighbors. As Iraq became increasingly sure of itself, conscious of its interests, and reticent to give way to outsiders, it began to violently pit itself against other nations, ultimately becoming one of the most notorious aggressors in the region.

Under the secular Baath Party and particularly under Saddam Hussein, who officially began his rule in 1979, Iraq rose from weakness and indifference to become a true challenger to Iranian power in the Middle East. The invasions of Iran in 1980 and then Kuwait in 1990 cemented Iraq's image as an expansive state ready and willing to engage its neighbors in combat.

When the United States invaded and occupied Iraq in 2003, few wept for the Iraqi dictator, whose hands had been drenched in Iraqi, Iranian, and Kuwaiti blood. The images of Kurdish victims falling prey to

Saddam's chemical weapons offensives in 1987 and 1988 and the constant reminder of Shia uprisings mercilessly crushed in 1991 made the idea of an occupation in the heart of the Middle East easier for an idealistic American public to stomach. Europeans cried foul, claiming that oil was behind George W. Bush's decision to go to war, while other critics pointed to the administration's desire to have permanent bases in the Middle East, especially since Saudi Arabia had been politely asking U.S. troops to leave.

For the neoconservatives who occupied the White House, however, the war was about democracy: democracy promotion and the fight against the elusive enemy of Islamic extremism. That Saddam was a secular pan-Arabist and an enemy on al-Qaeda's target list did not seem to matter. In fact, little in terms of logical reasoning appeared to be at play.

Some will disagree with the characterization of neoconservatives as mere idealists. American actions in Iraq have often been painted as plunder disguised as crusading. Veteran journalist Naomi Klein puts it thus: "Even their most committed critics tend to portray the neocons as true believers, motivated exclusively by a commitment to the supremacy of American and Israeli power that is so all-consuming they are prepared to sacrifice economic interests in favor of 'security.' This distinction is both artificial and amnesiac. The right to limitless profit-seeking has always been at the center of neocon ideology."[1] Klein rightly points out that neoconservative think tanks that beat their war drums the loudest before the invasion, namely the American Enterprise Institute and the Heritage Foundation, have taken a dogmatic stance on the infallibility of free markets and other "business-friendly" positions. No-bid contracts in Iraq were infamously awarded to Halliburton, the company previously run by Vice President Dick Cheney. The zealous and largely irrational push for the privatization of postwar Iraq has also done little to temper these skeptical viewpoints.

While the war's underlying motives may never be fully understood, the academic and largely useless term "weapons of mass destruction" (WMDs) became the conflict's selling point. Iraq's fate soon degenerated into the false dichotomy of whether Iraq had WMDs or not, with the media and the American public rarely asking what exactly the term meant and why it should be considered of serious, long-term consequence to American interests.

The kind of chemical weapons most believed Saddam Hussein had in his arsenal have been rendered cumbersome and of little value in either battlefield or terrorist scenarios (as both the Iran-Iraq War and the 1995 sarin gas attack by terror group Aum Shinrikyo on the Tokyo subway attest).[2] Anthrax, a biological weapon that Saddam was also believed to possess before the war, acts principally as a chemical agent, since it is noncommunicable and is rendered nonlethal with proper treatment. And the idea that Saddam had a working nuclear weapons program (a real "weapon of mass destruction") was based on the fruitless concept of trying to prove a negative (i.e., Iraq must prove it does *not* have weapons), as well as on "evidence" that amounted to the procurement of aluminum tubes, which only a *single* analyst within the intelligence community[3] was adamant could be used to manufacture uranium enrichment centrifuges, themselves not a guarantee of successful enrichment, let alone weaponization capabilities.

But the WMDs, the supposed reason the Unites States invaded and occupied a hostile country the size of France, were themselves never found. The Iraq invasion soon became a war without a cause, yet it was replete with long-term consequences we have only begun to grasp, not the least of which is the tipping of the balance of power in the region in favor of Iran, and the response from around the region, which is still being felt in Iraq in the form of sectarian attacks.

1920

The founding of modern Iraq has been nothing short of an exercise in expedient colonialism. The Ottomans, distrustful of Iranian influence, favored Sunnis over Shias, and this led to the artificial power of the former over the latter. Though they lived in Iraq's oil-rich, port-accessible fertile lands, Shias were often treated as second-class citizens right up until the 2003 invasion.

It should be noted that Middle Eastern history holds plenty of examples of minority rule. The Fatimids of Egypt were Ismaili Shias who governed over a mostly Sunni population. The Mamluks were a Turkish slave class that came to wield significant power over its Arab subjects. Ottoman Sunni rule over the Basra, Baghdad, and Mosul provinces, however, did not constitute minority rule until tribes in southern Iraq began to convert to Shiism in large numbers in the nineteenth century, substantially shifting the region's demographics.

Needless to say, the dramatic shift of Mesopotamia from majority Sunni to majority Shia did little to compel the Ottomans to work with the clergy in the holy cities. Instead, it only solidified their distrust of Iran and nudged them to continue granting preference, in jobs and educational opportunities, to their Sunni coreligionists. But what began as an exercise in regional power plays by the Ottomans eventually degenerated into an outright British fumble.

The British sought to keep the Sunnis in power over the Shias for a number of reasons. First, a policy of political continuity is easier to manage. The elite stratum was already in place when the British arrived in Iraq, and it would have taken nothing short of a revolutionary program to put Iraqi Shias on par with Sunnis in terms of educational and bureaucratic expertise.

Second, the British were keen to pursue a divide-and-conquer strategy that would ensure the smaller group of elites would have to depend on British firepower and finances to stave off a popular insurrection. This strategy is right out of a typical colonialist playbook, and it is responsible for a series of tragic postcolonial episodes, among them the Rwandan genocide of 1994.

Last, the British had their own reasons for keeping neighboring Shia Iran weak, and weakening Iraqi Shias could only help in this endeavor. Britain was concerned about Iranian power because of its own history in Iran. Iran had never been colonized by a European power, but starting in the mid-nineteenth century it had lain at the mercy of overt British and Russian influence. With Iran shifting to a new, more assertive dynasty under military strongman Reza Khan, Britain had a reason to keep its ambitions in check, if only for the sake of its already vast commercial interests in that country.

The British did more than empower Sunnis over Shias. Apart from stoking sectarian disharmony, tribalism became part and parcel of the British legacy in the region. Traditionally, Arab life had been centered on a degree of egalitarianism, in which "chiefs were invariably peers among equals, who did not issue orders as much as formulate a general consensus."[4] But from its earliest ventures in the region, starting in the seventeenth century, Britain had strengthened the hand of tribal leaders as a means of more easily negotiating treaties and keeping an administrative eye on the ground. Most notably, the British inflated the authority of tribal sheikhs in what is now the United Arab Emirates, so that these societies were no longer based on traditional, Arab tribal consensus but rather propped-up individuals reaching the level of autocrats.

The British repeated this formula in Iraq in the twentieth century. When the Mesopotamian Expeditionary Force entered the country in 1914, "individuals were picked out by the British intelligence services to act as tribal sheikhs, and were officially invested with juridical, and later financial, authority over their tribes."[5] At times the selection of individuals reflected a true hierarchy on the ground; at times it was purely arbitrary. Britain had little patience for long-winded tribal council meetings and the confusion over power sharing. Arab tribalism, thus, eventually became something it had never been: authoritarian. (It should be noted that the United States is revisiting this strategy with the Sunni Awakening, a movement to artificially empower local tribal leaders to aid in the fight against al-Qaeda. As we will see, the longterm repercussions of this approach may not yield staility. In the short term, however, it may be the only card that America has to curb the lawlessness.)

It should be emphasized that British diplomatic officials understood the social minefield of Iraq, as well as the persistent dilemma associated with trying to rule a country divided along sectarian lines. Internal strife within the diplomatic corps mainly split along two camps, those who wanted to keep a tight leash around the political and social developments of the country, and those who favored relative autonomy for the Iraqi people. This latter policy had been advocated by more liberal-minded bureaucrats such as Sir Arthur Hirtzel of the India Office, and legendary figures like T. E. Lawrence, of *Lawrence of Arabia* fame, and Gertrude Bell, whose official title of Oriental Secretary did not betray her monumental role in creating the modern state of Iraq.

Bell was lobbying to grant self-determination to the Iraqis sooner rather than later, not so much for ideological reasons, but for practical ones. She had traveled throughout the Arab world, dined with the Bedouin, lived in Iran, and even translated the poetry of Hafez into English. Bell understood the Middle East and particularly the underlying pride associated with independence. And although there was little to speak of in terms of Mesopotamian nationalism in 1920 Iraq, Bell knew that the desire of local Arabs to rid themselves of foreign meddling would take hold and force out the British sooner or later, especially since the British had done so much to stoke the flames of anticolonialism to begin with.

As two of the most active, influential, and respected officers in the fledgling British intelligence corps, Bell and Lawrence had gone to great lengths to personally convince Arab tribes to rise up against the Ottoman Turks, exactly on the grounds that being ruled by foreigners was an indignity. But with the Sykes-Picot Agreement, which had divvied up the Middle East between France and Britain, Bell and Lawrence were made to carry out a duplicitous policy that was compatible with neither their personal feelings nor their political outlook.

As the First World War came to an end, the directives from London were to remain in Mesopotamia until the Iraqis could stand on their own. Once statehood was set in place, the British would be free to leave. Of course, staying in the meantime only meant more light-handed colonialism, something that was hardly welcome after so many promises of self-determination.

On the opposite side of the liberals' self-rule ideals, and London's middle-ground colonial policy, were administrators like Arnold Wilson, who served as acting civil commissioner in Mesopotamia. In 1919 he sent a cable to the India Office warning of the dangers of a semiautonomous Iraq, on the grounds that by ceding control to the Iraqis too soon, Britain would essentially be granting the Sunnis an upper hand in perpetuity.

After all, the Sunni elite was the only community that came close to being able to administer the large country. Shias and Kurds, in contrast, had simply been marginalized too long to be able to step in. "[Any] attempts to introduce institutions on the lines desired by the Sunni politicians of Syria," wrote Arnold Wilson in retort to the light intervention policy, "would involve the concentration of power in the hands of a few persons whose ambitions and methods would rapidly bring about the collapse of organized government. The results would be the antithesis of democratic government."[6]

What Wilson was advocating then was the type of overt British involvement seen in India: the heavy colonial hand. Despite being based on the racist assumption that Indians could not handle the affairs of their own country, direct British administrative efforts, which included building the famed railroads, yielded an infrastructural and institutional gift that arguably has kept on giving, most evident in the existence of a populous, multisectarian and mutliethnic democracy in India.

But the loud echo of self-determination, unfavorable public opinion back in Britain, the rise of Arab nationalism, and the mere cost associated with holding colonies made Wilson's plan of heavy-handed intervention a nonstarter. Iraq would have to be influenced by Britain, but at least on the surface it had to appear to be ruled by Arabs. It is only unfortunate that the United States trod a similar road in 2003. It established a weak, ungovernable democracy with a limited American face to it (i.e., very few troops on the ground) after undertaking the most undemocratic of actions: the invasion of a country and the deposition of its leadership by unprovoked force. Ultimately, the tragedy of such contradictions has less to do with rhetorical hypocrisy than with the structural problems that such schizophrenic policies bring about.

The British pursued the middle-ground approach, and in 1921 King Faisal, a Hashemite Arabian who had been advanced to the Syrian throne and then promptly removed by France just a few months prior, was made King of Iraq. Certainly, he was no Iraqi, but then again, nobody was. Faisal was elected with 96 percent of the vote, a phony figure to be sure.

As do most placeholder leaders who are brought to power by external forces, Faisal had little success shoring up his local support base. At the end of the day, he was an agent of Britain, not a leader with any significant claim to legitimacy. "I undertake to be guided by your advice in all matters," Faisal told the British in a closed-door meeting. He understood more than anyone else that his fate rested on that of his benefactors. "H.M. Government and I are in the same boat and must sink or swim together. . . . Were instrument to fail and in consequence [Britain] left Iraq, I should have to leave too."[7]

This line could have been written by Iraqi prime minister Nouri al-Maliki and addressed to the U.S. Department of Defense. As did Faisal, many current Iraqi politicians will likely leave after the United States withdraws from Iraq. Those who remain will do so at great risk, given the fact that despite winning elections, they were hardly legitimate to begin with.

Faisal's figurative reign lasted twelve years, but in the interim Iraqi political life was beginning to take shape. Varying ideologies, ranging from Iraqi nationalism to communism took hold of the country. The monarchy began to wane, and expectations of self-determination choked Britain into eventual resignation. But self-rule, in the real sense of the word, had been sabotaged by the makeup of the Iraqi civil service as both the Ottomans and British had established it. With the absence of the Shia, who by all accounts made up the majority of the population, there was little in terms of a foundation for a stable country.

It should be noted that Shias were continually absent from Iraqi civil service in large part because of their self-exclusion. While many Sunni civil servants had come out of the Ottoman tradition of militarism and were increasingly entrenched secular elites, the Shia leadership came mostly from the clerical class. This distinction is owing to a number of reasons, a couple of which should be pointed out here.

Because the rank of grand ayatollah is attained naturally, through the accolades and following of students and the respect and admiration of colleagues, grand ayatollahs are leaders before they ever achieve a title. Regardless of whether an ayatollah is a quietist or activist cleric, in the political sense of the words, he will not need a government salary to generate a base of support, as he will make his living through khums revenues.

In addition, the Shia had a generally complicated relationship with the new Iraq. Many leading clerics were not only connected to Iran religiously but were of Iranian stock. The names of prominent ayatollahs alone betray their origin because they often take as a surname the name of the city from which they hail. Ayatollah Ali al-Sistani hails from Sistan, Iran, while the historic leader of the 1920 revolt against the British, Muhammad Taqi al-Shirazi, comes from Shiraz, Iran (and was a disciple of Grand Ayatollah Muhammad Mirza Hasan Shirazi, who in 1891 helped lead the Tobacco Protest aimed at British interests in Iran). As Vali Nasr writes, up to "75 percent of the population of Karbala was Iranian" around the time that Iraq became a modern state.[8] Iranian Shias, then, had little incentive then to work toward the continuation of Sunni-domination over a country created by British administrators just a few months prior.

This notwithstanding, Faisal did make some overtures to the Shia during his reign. In the early 1920s, as the British were attempting to sign a treaty with Iraq to cement their influence over the country's political and economic affairs, Faisal gave the path of sovereignty a try. If he could unite the Shia, who at that time made up around 55 percent of the population (as opposed to the 22 percent Sunnis and 14 percent Kurds) behind him, then Faisal had a real shot at asserting Iraqi unity, and perhaps ultimately independence. For the most part, however, the Shia reacted with suspicion and refused to join his experiment.

Saddam's Rise

In 1956 Egyptian president Gamal Abdel Nasser nationalized the Suez Canal, prompting a joint invasion by Great Britain, France, and Israel. After the three countries stood down under pressure from the United States, Nasser emerged the true victor. Preaching pan-Arabism, an ideology that sought to unite Arab countries under one state, Nasser soon became the darling of the Arab world, giving hope to millions who had suffered the indignities of colonial rule, repression, and the birth of the modern state of Israel.

In 1958 Egypt and Syria merged into a single state, the United Arab Republic (UAR). In this new country, Nasser played a leading role with the active support of a pan-Arab organization called the Baath, or "Renaissance," Party of Syria. Pan-Arabism, at its core, was a secular ideology that focused on ethnic unity over religious differences. As such, pan-Arabists were less concerned with who was Sunni or Shia, or even whether members were Muslim at all. The goal was unity under a single cultural and linguistic narrative. Michel Aflaq, the best known of the Baath Party's three cofounders was himself a Christian, of Greek Orthodox faith. Through Aflaq's work, the Baath Party embraced the UAR as a vehicle to expel their Communist rivals from Syria and set the wheels in motion for a singular Arab state.

Back in Iraq, the Hashimite monarchy feared the worst. The king (now Faisal II) imagined Soviet-backed pan-Arabs arriving at his doorstep and so he ordered his relatively weak military to march toward Jordan in the hopes that it could buffer any potential aggression coming from Lebanon and Syria, where Nasserism was beginning to take off in earnest. Instead, a group of free officers in the Iraqi air force, led by Abd al-Karim Qasim, staged a *coup d'état* that ended with the king's execution. The monarchy ended in 1958, but the pan-Arabists had not yet triumphed.

Qasim, who eventually surfaced from obscurity to become president of the newly founded Republic of Iraq, did not automatically become a vehicle for Nasser's rise. Instead, he aligned with the Communists, who had been gaining considerable traction with the growth of a powerful labor movement in Iraq. Iraqi Baathists soon countered with movements of their own, which "consisted largely of gangs of thugs" led by such figures as a young Saddam Hussein.[9] Baathists and Communists engaged in bloody street battles reminiscent of Berlin's Weimar-era fistfights between the Nazis of the far right, and the Communists of the far left, leading to a polarized conflict that only hardened identities and made the eventual winners all the more unforgiving.

As was the case with just about everything in Iraq, belonging to the political left or right came with sectarian implications. The Shia had traditionally been associated with the Communist Party, and the strongmen of the Baath Party with Sunnism. When Ahmad Hasan al-Bakr, the future president of Iraq, staged a brief anticommunist coup in 1963, it was aimed at moving key political figures from the so-called Sunni Triangle of western Iraq into positions of influence within the intelligence services. For their part, the Shia suffered a deadly barrage of political killings in the name of anticommunist purges.

Though he had been pushed out just a few months after the first coup, Colonel al-Bakr returned with another coup in 1968, this time establishing the Baath Party as the leading political force in the country. His cousin Saddam Hussein acted as the new president's henchman, doing much of the dirty work in the form of death warrants and torture aimed at Bakr's political enemies.

Saddam was an able political operative, and he soon outwitted and marginalized al-Bakr, his own mentor, forcing him to officially resign in July 1979. That year Saddam assembled around four hundred Baath operatives for a long-winded party congress. Footage from the event shows how Saddam ghoulishly and in real time purged the government of all potential threats. Standing at the podium, he quietly called the names of key party officials and accused each of betrayal. As the names were called, the accused stood quietly and walked away into oblivion, escorted out of the massive hall by the regime's feared security detail. In the aftermath of the spectacle, secret trials were held and as many as five hundred people were put to death.[10] Saddam and his closest associates served as personal executioners.

The Baath Party had largely started as a family affair, with most high-ranking officials hailing from Saddam's Beijat clan of the Albu Nasr tribe in the Sunni Triangle. As the party grew, however, Saddam assembled a formidable enterprise, with active party cells springing up in towns and villages across the country. At its height in the late 1980s, up to 10 percent of the population belonged to the party, including many Shia, who made up the majority of the ranks. Seeking the financial opportunities that came with officially joining the party, the Shia were nevertheless unable to break through and hold any sway over the regime, which remained Sunni-dominated until Saddam's fall in 2003.

The Shia Families

The 1958 coup had a profound impact on Shia political life in Iraq. Shiism had seen a decline in khums revenues, resulting in economic stagnation in the holy cities. Ayatollahs watched their student bases dwindle, as young people were increasingly attracted to the emerging secular political movements of the day, namely nationalism, communism, and even Baathism.

As the secular movements were taking hold in Iraq, Shia theologians were hardly silent. Throughout the Iraqi Republic's existence, two influential families garnered most of the attention. They drew their political legitimacy from their religious credentials, their following on the street, and their activist, revolutionary ideology. These were the Sadr and Hakim factions. These two families have made political waves largely through their rejection of a quietist (i.e., nonpolitical) ideology.

The Sadr family has had a profound impact, not only in Iraq, but also in Iran, Lebanon, and beyond. During the 1920 revolution, Ismail Sadr, the grandfather of Iraq's famed Muhammad Baqir al-Sadr, played a key role in the anti-British uprisings of southern Iraq. Ismail's other grandson, Musa al-Sadr, was the founder of the Lebanese Amal organization, a precursor and eventual competitor of Hezbollah, in 1975.

Muhammad Baqir (1935–80) is considered a pioneer in Shia political activism. He belonged to a group of clerics who called for an active role in social movements, in sharp contrast with the quietist trend that the majority high-ranking seminarians advocated. In 1957, in the midst of the massive wave of Arab nationalism, Baqir formed the Islamic Dawa Party, a revolutionary movement that continued to operate through the years of Baath Party rule and became one of the ruling parties of post-2003 Iraq (with Prime Minister Nouri al-Maliki as a leading member).

As the Iranian Revolution was coming to a close in February 1979 and Ruhollah Khomeini's stock was rising, Baqir flirted with the idea of pushing for his own revolution in Iraq. He sent representatives to meet with Khomeini, but he never "pulled the trigger," in the figurative sense. Even if he had, there is little reason to believe that Khomeini would have ever assisted Sadr considering his own preoccupations with consolidating power at home. The events of early 1979 also coincided with Saddam's rise to power, and before long, the ability to stage a bona fide revolution was severely hampered. On June 12, Baqir was taken into custody by the Baath regime.

In some ways, Baqir could see the limitations of an Iranian-style revolution, even though he was an early supporter. Commenting on the writings of his colleague Khomeini, who had taught alongside him while in exile in Najaf, Baqir expressed misgivings about the concept of wilayat al-faqih (Khomeini's doctrine of 'Rule by the Jurisprudent') and how it might be applicable in a modern state. In wilayat al-faqih, Khomeini had looked to place the leadership of a modern state in the hands of a single qualified jurist, and this did not sit well with Baqir's philosophy.

Baqir suggested that the powers bestowed on clerics were not limitless. He warned that ijtihad did not constitute lawmaking in itself, but rather was merely a potential source for it—one that in practicality is not equal to the Qur'an and the oral traditions of the Imams.[11] By saying this, he implied that Khomeini could be overstepping the boundaries of clerical authority.

Despite the differences of opinion between Baqir and Khomeini, Baqir's writings continued to be influential in Iran in the revolution's aftermath, and his vision of an Islamic state, which was circulated widely in Arabic and Persian throughout Iran, was eventually worked into the Iranian constitution.[12] Baqir insisted that "the people are the possessors of the right to implement" both legislative and executive powers. And while Khomeini's vision of an all-powerful executive, fashioned largely after Plato's philosopher-king archetype in *The Republic*,[13] would act as the top layer of power in Iran, an inner structure of republican separation of powers (as advocated by Baqir) was also written into the constitution, allowing for the election of a president, and the democratization of the parliament, which had been tightly controlled by the shah. Although these institutions are systematically abused and manipulated by the Islamic

Republic's ruling elite, the new constitution gave Iran a more democratic-leaning system than any other it has had in its 2,500-year history.[14]

Baqir's contributions to Islamic politics soon ended. On April 8, 1980, he was executed along with his sister Bint al-Huda in retaliation for a wave of anti-Baathist violence in Iraq. It is said that Saddam's agents made Baqir watch his sister's rape before the agents hammered a nail into his skull. Both Baqir and Bint al-Huda were later hanged.

Baqir's nephew, Muhammad Muhammad Sadiq al-Sadr (1943–99), took up the mantle of Baqir's partisans. Though Sadiq worked with the regime to act as a state-sanctioned community leader in the 1990s, and thus fell from grace in the eyes of some Shia activists, his work with the government was done to help the poor in the midst of postwar sanctions and, just as important, to spread confidence among the faithful. Soon, Sadr came to represent a quintessentially Iraqi Shia voice, one that had gotten louder and more assertive following the Iran-Iraq War and the mercilessly crushed Shia uprising at the hand of Saddam Hussein in 1991, which resulted in over 150,000 deaths (and which Iran and the United States all but ignored). Both events had the effect of widening the gap between Iraqi Shias and Iran, and created a more insulated community that learned to rely on itself or survival. Ultimately, Sadr's popular appeal in the midst of a growing number of active Shias was too much for the regime to handle, and it ordered his murder in 1999.

When Saddam's government fell in 2003, the Shia slums of eastern Baghdad, al-Thawra (also called Saddam City), were renamed Sadr City in honor of the fallen Sadiq. His son Muqtada (b. 1973) inherited his loyal throngs of followers. Despite being a lousy public speaker of limited religious study, Muqtada continued in a long tradition of Islamic leaders who successfully channeled the charismatic authority of their predecessors by becoming a de facto leader of the Sadrist movement in Iraq.

One family that came to both work with, and ultimately break away from, the Sadrs, was the powerful House of Hakim. Muhsin al-Hakim (1889–1970), the family's elder, established himself in the 1960s as a venerable force in the Shia community by becoming Iraq's sole, or preeminent marja, an honor of being the ultimate, go-to ayatollah that was later held by Grand Ayatollah Abu al-Qasem al-Khoei, and most recently by Grand Ayatollah Ali al-Sistani. Like both Khoei and Sistani, Muhsin pursued a quietist approach to politics, and as such he avoided many of the formative battles regarding Arab nationalism and Shia activism. His decisions, however, did have a profound political impact on Shia communities, both locally and abroad. The Dawa Party came to fruition through Muhsin's blessing, and Muhsin also recommended that Musa al-Sadr, the founder of Amal, travel to Lebanon to help the Shia community there better assert itself on the eve of the Lebanese civil war.

Unlike the elder al-Hakim, however, sons Muhammad Baqir (1939–2003) and Abdul Aziz (b. 1953) became stalwart supporters of the politically active wing of the Iraqi Shia community. After the death of Baqir al-Sadr in 1980, Muhammad Baqir al-Hakim fled to Syria, and ultimately Iran, where he helped found the Supreme Council of the Islamic Revolution in Iraq (SCIRI). SCIRI's use of force on behalf of Iran against Iraq during the eight-year war put a strain on an already competitive relationship between the Sadrs and Hakims. It was seen, after all, as an abandonment of the Iraqi people on behalf of Iran. And to this day, the Hakims are remembered as the group that avoided many of the perils of life under Saddam, particularly during the Shia uprisings in the Gulf War's aftermath and under the heavy weight of punishing UN sanctions.

Yet the Hakims did not fully escape Saddam's reach. In response to the formation of SCIRI, dozens of al-Hakim's relatives and associates were systematically murdered by the regime. One of his brothers, Mahdi, was killed by Saddam's agents while attending a conference in the Sudan.[15] For Baqir al-Hakim, there was no going back to Iraq—not until Saddam was gone.

A New Balance of Power

The dualism of eastern and western empires in the Middle East began to wane in the seventeenth century as two developments took hold of the region. One was the implosion of the Safavid Empire, a process that ended with an Afghan invasion of Iran in 1722. The other key development was the entrance of European powers into the region. By the mid-1800s, the region was a massive power vacuum. In Iran, Russia fought Britain for control, while the dwindling Ottoman Empire lost many of its territories, including Egypt and the then mostly symbolic Arabian Peninsula (oil was not tapped until the 1930s).

The defeat of the Central Powers in the First World War meant the collapse of the "old" empires of Austria-Hungary and the Ottomans. The spoils were divided among Britain and France, which, amid the fervor of rising Arab and Turkish nationalism drew lines in the sand to make up "countries." These states were born largely as mandates of the League of Nations and were to be "protected" by European powers. Non-Arab countries Iran and Turkey were themselves never colonized, and were thus spared some of the humiliation.

In the context of the Cold War, and more specifically starting with the Johnson administration, America came to depend on Iran and Saudi Arabia as de facto strongmen to fight communism in the region. Under Nixon, this came to be called the "twin-pillar" policy, and it only grew in importance given the Nixon Doctrine's reliance on regional powers to provide local security. America, however, was "to rely primarily on Iran, since Saudi Arabia was considered too weak to enforce regional stability and security, a role which Iran could play."[16]

In Iran, the United States propped up the government of Mohammad Reza Pahlavi, providing billions in weapons in addition to what seemed like limitless political support, including the infamous 1953 CIA-staged coup, which toppled the shah's political nemesis, democratically elected premier Mohammad Mosaddeq. But if America had created a friendly powerhouse in the region, it didn't diligently keep tabs on developments inside Iran. Instability was brewing and discontent with the shah's heavy-handed ways (and by extension, his foreign benefactors) soon reached the boiling point.

The Iranian Revolution of 1978–79 was a wakeup call to the United States, as well as a game-changing shift in the region's balance of power. The anti-American tone of the revolution, which finally forced the shah out on January 16, 1979, was a call to nonalignment in a world divided between America and the Soviet Union. Arab countries began fearing the worst from Iran, as Ayatollah Khomeini, the spiritual leader and eventual winner of the postrevolutionary power struggle, called for the exportation of what he termed the "Islamic" Revolution.

Saddam Hussein saw the Iranian Revolution's aftermath as a perfect opportunity to expand his country's influence as a leader in the Arab world, while at the same time he consolidated his rule at home. On September 22, 1980, Saddam ordered a surprise attack on ten Iranian military airfields along the Iraqi border. Competing claims over the oil-rich Shatt al-Arab delta had fueled the conflict, but Iran's isolating revolution provided Saddam with the only credible opportunity to attack.

With the end of American support for Iran, the balance of power in the Middle East was up for grabs. Without a clear sense of what constituted stability, Saddam imagined a region under Arab leadership, with Iraq steering the course. In setting up his country as the leader of Arab nationalism, Saddam harkened back to the Abbasid caliphate and the Golden Age of Islam, fashioning himself as Caliph Mansur, the founder of Baghdad, whose adopted name meant "the victorious." At the height of the war a leading Iraqi newspaper named Baghdad "The City of the Two Mansurs."[17]

The basis for the Iran-Iraq War was a prior agreement that had left Iraq with a bitter taste. Back in 1975, Iraq had abandoned claims over the Shatt al-Arab with the Algiers Agreement. The truce with Iran came as a result of Saddam's military campaign against Kurdistan Democratic Party rebels in the north, which were then being supplied with weaponry by the United States and Israel, but especially Iran. Through Algiers, Saddam finally persuaded Iran to cut aid to the Kurds, but in the process he "apparently lost an unfought war against Iran" over the disputed territories, which straddled the southern portion of the Iran-Iraq border.[18]

After the Iranian Revolution was over, however, Iran underwent a period of factionalism and chaos. Thousands of Iranians died in the ensuing power struggle, and the shah's armed forces, once funded by the United States to act as a lynchpin of regional, anticommunist security, were systematically and brutally purged by the emerging regime.

By the fall of 1980, fifty-two American hostages were still being held by Iran in connection with the 1979 seizure of the U.S. embassy in Tehran, all part of a jostling for internal control of the country. The new Islamic Republic, which was increasingly coming under the thumb of Khomeini, had few allies left, and if Saddam wanted his hands on the oil-rich Shatt al-Arab, he had to act fast. Although Iran was caught off guard by the invasion, Khomeini was able to use the war to mobilize public opinion in his favor. Soon, even some of the cleric's most brutal enemies took up arms in defense of Iran, a country that had three times the population and several times the gross domestic product of Iraq.

For its part, Iraq enjoyed the support of most of its Arab neighbors, along with both superpowers, who wanted to end Iran's experiment with political nonalignment. The result, however, was an emboldened Iran fighting against an artificially powerful Iraq—a recipe for bloody stalemate. Once the dust had settled on the eight-year war, one million lay dead on both sides, and no real changes had been made to the map.

If the Iran-Iraq War had a unifying effect on Iranian society, it similarly fomented nationalism in Iraq. Shias, weary of Saddam Hussein and tired of Sunni domination, nevertheless found themselves fighting against their fellow Shia in defense of their country. Certainly, Saddam's dictatorial hand played a role. Any soldier who refused to fight would be executed on the spot, his family charged for the bullet that killed him. Iran, which engaged in its own brutality, did not treat its fellow Shia of Iraq kindly when they were captured on the battlefield. During the war, Iraqis became Iraqis, and Iranians remained Iranians.[19]

After the Iran-Iraq War, Saddam rebuilt his armed forces once again, this time setting his sights on neighboring Kuwait—a country that Iraq had claimed as its own territory since 1920 and that the Saddam accused of slant drilling into Iraqi oil reserves. That Iraq owed Kuwait billions in war debt only helped Saddam's resolve, and on August 2, 1990, he invaded.

When the United States mobilized a coalition with over a half million troops to liberate Kuwait, Saddam's regime began to suffer under an immense weight of defeat. Cracks began to show. In early March 1991 throngs of Shia faithful rose up in southern Iraq, yelling anti-Saddam slogans and sacking Baath Party offices; anyone associated with the regime was targeted, fellow Shia included. Patrick Cockburn recounts,

> In Kerbala, to the north of Najaf, Sanaa Mohammaed, a Shia government employee, was astonished at the speed with which the regime was disintegrating around her. ... Almost immediately, revenge killings began. "Two members of the Baath party were killed in our street," says Sanaa. "My family and I were terrified because my brothers worked in government jobs, so they fled from Kerbala. ... I saw a middle-aged man, in the sort of suit that Baath party members used to wear, running down the street until he was out of breath, with two or three men chasing him firing their guns. ... They threw his corpse onto a pile of bodies of people who had been killed earlier in the day."[20]

By March 5 the Kurds too rose up, and the previously oppressed groups began to look for the United States for help in finishing the job. The United States didn't come, and neither did Iran, which had been funding the largest and best-organized opposition groups in Iraq, yet didn't want to overplay its hand. The Shia and the Kurds were left to Saddam's revenge, and up to 150,000 Shia were murdered by the regime in retaliation for the uprising.

The United States had reasons not too support the Shia revolts, and it stood firm against the idea of "marching all the way to Baghdad" and ousting Saddam Hussein. President George H. W. Bush thought it prudent at the time to avoid the kind of popular chaos that might lead to an Iranian-style, Shia revolution in Iraq. After all, Iran had been bankrolling the most powerful opposition forces inside the country, and regime change from the bottom up would almost certainly put Iran in the driver's seat of Iraq's future. Instead, as Cockburn suggests, the first Bush administration wanted regime change to occur in the form of a coup, the way such transfers of power had taken place throughout Iraq's young history. Zalmay Khalilzad, director of policy planning at the State Department, wrote, "Iraqi disintegration will improve prospects for Iranian domination of the Gulf and remove a restraint on Syria."[21] But perhaps the most articulate position against the invasion and occupation of Iraq was presented by Dick Cheney, who in a strange twist of fate would later become one of the biggest advocates of the U.S. invasion of Iraq. In a 1994 interview with C-SPAN, Cheney defended George H. W. Bush's unwillingness to march on Baghdad at the close of the 1991 Gulf War. Cheney said:

> [If] we'd gone to Baghdad we would have been all alone. There wouldn't have been anybody else with us. There would have been a U.S. occupation of Iraq. None of the Arab forces that were willing to fight with us in Kuwait were willing to invade Iraq. Once you got to Iraq and took it over, took down Saddam Hussein's government, then what are you going to put in its place? That's a very volatile part of the world, and if you take down the central government of Iraq, you could very easily end up seeing pieces of Iraq fly off—part of it the Syrians would like to have to the west, part of eastern Iraq the Iranians would like to claim, fought over it for eight years. In the north you've got the Kurds, and if the Kurds spin loose and join with the Kurds in Turkey, then you threaten the territorial integrity of Turkey. It's a quagmire if you go that far and try to take over Iraq. The other thing was casualties. Everyone was impressed with the fact we were able to do our job with as few casualties as we had. But for the 146 Americans killed in action, and for their families, it wasn't a cheap war. And the question for the president, in terms of whether or not we went on to Baghdad, took additional casualties in an effort to get Saddam Hussein, was how many additional dead Americans is Saddam worth? Our judgment was, not very many, and I think we got it right.[22]

Throughout the 1990s, the United States pursued a policy of dual containment, whereby both Iran and Iraq were contained through sanctions and political isolation. Iraq, which suffered under multilateral sanctions and whose airspace was largely restricted by UN-mandated "No Fly Zones," was naturally the weaker of the two parties. For a brief moment, this careful balance of power (rather a "balance of weakness," as Jalil

Roshandel has called it[23]) seemed to have the desired effect of calming the traditional Middle Eastern rivalries.

Iraq went from spending $20.2 billion on defense at the height of the Iran-Iraq War in 1985, to $8.6 billion in 1990, and a meager $1.2 billion in 1997 (all figures in 2004 U.S. dollars). By 2002, when the United States was making a case for war, Iraq was spending only $2.3 billion on defense, Iran was spending twice as much, and Saudi Arabia nearly eight times that amount.[24]

Iran was relatively contained but not overtly threatened during the 1990s, and it was during this period that it elected (1997) and reelected (2001) President Mohammad Khatami, a reformist running on a platform of improved relations with the United States. It was in part the stability of dual containment, which seemed to provide Iranian moderates with the kind of cover necessary to start engaging with the world. Case in point was a 2002 interview with CNN's Christiane Amanpour, in which Khatami came the closest any sitting Iranian president had to apologizing for the 1979–81 hostage crisis, saying in part, "I do know that the feelings of the great American people have been hurt, and of course I regret it."[25]

Certainly, not everyone in Washington perceived a balance of power in the Persian Gulf. Throughout the 1990s, U.S. policy hawks waged a public relations campaign for a more vigorous regime-change policy in Iraq. On January 26, 1998, a group of leading neoconservatives sent a letter to President Clinton urging him to pursue a strategy that "should aim, above all, at the removal of Saddam Hussein's regime from power."[26] Twelve of the eighteen signatories went on to occupy high-level posts in the George W. Bush administration, and they included future Secretary of Defense Donald Rumsfeld, Deputy Secretary of Defense Paul Wolfowitz, and even Zalmay Khalilzad.

Also in 1998, Bill Clinton was embroiled in a scandal over his sexual affair with White House intern Monica Lewinsky, and he appeared eager to focus the country's attention on Iraqi noncompliance with illicit weapons inspections. The Lewinsky scandal broke on January 17, and within a month, Bill Richardson, U.S. ambassador to the UN, became the face of a campaign to link Saddam Hussein with weapons of mass destruction. On February 11 Richardson told Margaret Warner of PBS, "Now, it reaches a point where you have to say, are we going to stand back and allow Saddam Hussein to get his way and continue developing these weapons of mass destruction, continue to threaten his neighbor, continue to gas the Kurds, continue to gas the Iranians, continue to be a threat to Israel, or are we going to simply say enough? ... Time is running out for Saddam Hussein."[27]

The link between Iraq and WMD continued to be the Clinton administration's focus throughout 1998, despite the fact that any evidence of the existence of illicit weapons programs dated back to the immediate aftermath of the 1991 Gulf War, with no subsequent verification of Iraq's possessing such research and development programs thereafter.[28] Although there was no clear evidence of an Iraqi chemical or biological program, no proof that Iraq would have an intention to use such weapons, and no proof that such weapons could ever be more effective than conventional explosives in inflicting casualties (not an insignificant point), the administration continued to hammer into the American consciousness the Saddam-WMD link, which the Bush administration later revived as the casus belli for the 2003 invasion.

In October Clinton signed into law the Iraq Liberation Act of 1998, a document that explicitly pursued regime change through the increased funding of opposition groups. And on the night of December 16, the United States and Great Britain began Operation Desert Fox, a four-day bombing campaign over Iraq that was ostensibly a response to Iraq having "kicked out" UN weapons inspectors. (In reality the inspectors had willingly withdrawn as a result of Iraq's limited compliance with their requests.) The next day the U.S. House of Representatives temporarily suspended its planned vote on Articles of Impeachment against Bill Clinton, which had been drawn up in the aftermath of the Lewinsky affair. It seemed that a renewed war in the Gulf had bought the president at some time.

When George W. Bush came to office, he brought with him a team of neoconservatives who had fanned the flames of war with Iraq throughout the 1990s, and more important, he inherited an American public that had been sold the idea that America's biggest threat was Iraq and its elusive (or nonexistent) weapons of mass destruction programs. Though few Americans could explain what WMDs were, let alone know that the kind used by Saddam had been proved to be of less potency than conventional weaponry, the fear campaign had its effect. On September 11, 2001, when al-Qaeda launched the most deadly terrorist attack ever perpetrated on the United States, the finger was promptly pointed at Saddam Hussein. Not two years later, the United States invaded and occupied Iraq.

7

THE FIRST IRAQ

Before there was post-war Iraq, there was the Lebanese civil war, an unforgiving, fifteen-year affair that gave birth to household names like the Lebanese Hezbollah and the Sabra and Shatila massacre. For the United States, the lessons not learned in 1980s Beirut continue to hit home. In Lebanon, as in Iraq, fleeting periods of calm have often given way to overconfidence and unwarranted optimism; and as in Iraq, political actors view their system as a zero-sum game, one that has to be carefully negotiated if a catastrophe is to be avoided.

Lebanon was born when France carved the country out of Syria in 1920, making it a Christian-led mandate under the name of Greater Lebanon. The idea was simple: by weakening Syria, France could more easily quell nationalist sentiment in its colonial possessions. But there was also a larger narrative behind the move to set up a nation of coreligionists with ties to Europe, one that harkened back to the Crusades several centuries prior.

The First Crusade was launched in 1095 by Pope Urban II, who used the military campaigns to focus an overpowering and destructive Christian militant energy toward an external enemy: Islam. The campaigns also provided Europe with a logical entry to the Silk Road in the East. By the eleventh century, what was left of the Byzantine Empire in Anatolia had already been weakened at the hand of the Seljuks, and after repeated calls from Constantinople, the papacy finally answered with military support. As the armies, largely made up of French conscripts, marched east, pogroms against Jews and rival Christian sects littered the fields of Europe and Anatolia. This was sectarian war.

Once in the region, the Crusaders set up fortresses from which they could attack the "infidels" and launch their siege, first on Antioch and later on Jerusalem. The wars were as much cultural as they were religious and political. Jews, Muslims, and even eastern Christians suffered under the same European onslaught and banded together to repel the foreign invaders. Eventually, Europe gave up, abandoning the repeated incursions into the region in the late thirteenth century.

The Crusades left behind deep scars of mistrust, shame, and indignity, and for the region's inhabitants, the invasions "have neither been forgotten nor forgiven."[1] Yet there was one faction that seemed to singly embrace the European invaders. The Maronite Christians, a sect of Catholicism founded in the fifth century, developed a fraternity with Europe over the centuries. Tucked away in Lebanon's mountains within an overwhelmingly Muslim region, the Maronites came to develop a bunker mentality vis-à-vis the surrounding communities. They often found themselves in a self-fulfilling prophecy of confrontation, fed on a legacy of Christian-Muslim violence in the region.

Beginning in the mid-nineteenth century, Maronites began to explain their cultural uniqueness by fashioning a narrative of Phoenician descent. The Phoenicians, the legendary Semitic civilization to whom both the West and the Middle East owe their systems of writing, were a convenient people to be attached to, given their ancient presence in the Levant. And their link to this ancient people placed the Maronites on the land before the Muslim armies marched into the region in the seventh century, helping foster a powerful, alternative narrative to Muslim identity.

The Phoenicians, a "race of seafaring mountaineers . . . a gift from heaven,"[2] at times provided Maronites with a conduit for feelings of superiority and an ideal of Lebanon in which Christianity was atop a social hierarchy. In the Maronite version of "democracy" their religion, nay, their particular sect of Christianity, represents the ultimate cultural, political, and social imagery of the country. To be Lebanese, then, is to embrace the Maronites.

The cultural connections between Christian Europe and the Maronite Levant also provided the religious enclave with another layer of separation from its surroundings. This connection to the outside was a fuse that at any time could spark a war, given the inherent and often irreconcilable divisions between Arab-Islamic culture and the European Crusaders, and later the colonialists.

Since the country was not formed in what one might call a "natural" fashion, it is no accident that factions have sought to stake their claims within its boundaries, and at times even the Maronites have wanted to secede and form their own state. Both the Palestine Liberation Organization (PLO) under Yasser Arafat and, more recently, the Lebanese Hezbollah, have founded what have been called "states within a state," essentially independently governed enclaves. Each of these enclaves had the dubious honor of having invited Israeli attacks suffered by the rest of the population.

The presence of Palestinian refugee camps and high-ranking PLO leadership in the late 1960s and 1970s was a source of chronic instability in Lebanon, and ultimately led to the civil war. To make matters worse, Israel was fighting a global campaign against the PLO at the time, so it considered its presence so close to home a threat and provocation. The Jewish state invaded Lebanon to oust the Palestinian organization, and finally in 1982 Arafat agreed to a U.S.-mediated disarmament and a departure from the country.

Today, the PLO is long gone from Lebanon, though many Palestinians have remained, unable to gain citizenship and mired in a stateless limbo. But while the Palestinian resistance has left Lebanon, another state within a state has emerged. A homegrown Shia movement known as the Lebanese Hezbollah, or "Party of God," has become much more disciplined and militarily powerful than the PLO ever was, and today it straddles the line between political faction and independent country.

In 1982 about fifteen hundred members of Iran's Islamic Revolutionary Guard Corps (IRGC) were sent to Lebanon to create, train, and arm Hezbollah. Ever since, Iran has offered a bulk of its funding, providing between $10 and 20 million to the organization per month.[3] This was part of Iran's regional strategy to break through the isolation generated by the Islamic Revolution. Yet Lebanese-Iranian cooperation was nothing new. Ever since the Safavids sought clerics from the Jabal Amil region of southern Lebanon to help them convert Iran into Shiism in the 1500s, cultural and religious ties have been strong between the two communities. The shah of Iran, for one, is known to have sent members of his security services, the SAVAK, to train and arm Shia militants to fight back against the Soviet-backed PLO. And the Shia Amal Movement was founded by Musa al-Sadr—a middle-ranking Iranian cleric and cousin of Iraq's Muqtada.

Like Khomeini of Iran, the highly charismatic Musa al-Sadr never confirmed or denied the rumor that he was an Imam, leaving it to the believer to decide how holy and infallible a man he really was. When he mysteriously disappeared from Libya in 1978, Musa only rose to greater mythical status, reminding believers of the Hidden Imam. (In reality, Musa is believed to have been assassinated by Libyan president Muammar Qaddafi.)

Musa al-Sadr continues to inspire reverence, though Amal has been upstaged by Hezbollah, whose "spiritual guide" is Grand Ayatollah Muhammad Husayn Fadlallah. Considered too liberal by some, Fadlallah cannot compete with the admiration inspired by Hezbollah's de facto political leader, the lower-ranking but significantly more powerful cleric, Sheikh Hasan Nasrallah. Nasrallah has merely the rank of hujjatu al-Islam, yet this does not preclude him from enjoying a massive following. On a recent trip to the *dahiye*, the Shia suburbs of South Beirut, I asked a Sunni wife of a high-ranking Lebanese military officer whether she had feared for her life during the Israeli bombing of July 2006. "I was afraid at first," she said. "But then Shaikh Nasrallah said he would protect us, and I wasn't afraid any more." The power is in the leader, not in an official title, or in this case even in a person's sectarian identity.

In the West, Hezbollah will forever be known as the organization that pioneered the use of suicide bombings in the Middle East. For the United States in particular, Hezbollah is remembered as the organization that attacked a U.S. Marine barracks in Beirut, killing 241 service members and forcing President Ronald Reagan to abandon peacekeeping operations in the Lebanese civil war.

Lebanon Ablaze

Like the post-2003 civil war in Iraq, the civil war in Lebanon could have been seen coming from a mile away, given the country's fractured, sectarian makeup. In fact, several turf battles had already rattled the region in the nineteenth century, with the most brutal fought between Maronites and the Druze, a fellow mountain-dwelling and reclusive sect that originated after the Fatimid Empire's defeat in Cairo.

Unlike Nizari Ismailis, who engaged in assassination campaigns during Mamluk and Mongol times, the Ismailis who eventually became the Druze preferred to keep to themselves and eventually came to shun conversion by outsiders into their group. As a result of their relative isolation, they developed a unique theology, which includes the belief in reincarnation, something that makes other Muslims uneasy and unwilling to accept them as part of the Islamic world.

Like the Maronites, the Druze's traditional distrust of other groups often put the community on heightened alert. This seemed like a natural fit with the insecure Christians of Lebanon, but the Maronites' high socioeconomic status bred resentment on the part of the Druze and soon mutual fears and distrust spilled over into violent conflict. In 1860 the secretive sect launched a bloody offensive on the Maronites, only compounding the Christians' feelings of persecution. The Maronites were massacred in large numbers, even inside their churches. This trauma was formative in the development of Maronite consciousness in Lebanon, and when they were given a chance to fashion a country from scratch with the help of Europe, they sought to it that their community define the terms of Lebanon's sectarian character.

On September 1, 1920, French General Henri Gouraud proclaimed the existence of the "State of Greater Lebanon," a French concoction based partly on Maronite ideas but more specifically on the immediate needs of the French Republic. "It was in defence of the presumed 'sovereignty' of this peculiar nation," Robert Fisk writes, "that countless thousands were to die more than half a century later."[4]

Because of the Maronites' strong footing in the country, they represented the economic and social elite from the very beginning. In the 1932 census (the only one ever taken), Christians comprised over 50 percent of the total population (31 percent of whom were Maronites), compared with 20 percent for the Sunnis, 18 percent for the Shia, and a mere 6.5 percent for the Druze.[5] By 1975, however, the situation looked much different. Muslims outnumbered Christians, and a sizable population of displaced Palestinians was seeking greater influence over the political affairs of the divided nation. Under the national pact, an unwritten rule that had shaped Lebanese politics since 1943, Maronites were to control the presidency, Sunnis the prime minister's office, and the relatively poor and politically weak Shias the post of speaker of the parliament.

As demography changed, Muslims became uneasy with the Christians' dominant position. By the time of the war, Christians had shrunk to "a little more than one-third of the population," with Muslims and Druze combined representing two-thirds.[6] A sectarian arms race ensued, with militias competing for foreign military support in their quest to defend themselves against one another. As often happens in such conflicts, it was the mistrust—the arms race itself—which led to a devastating civil war. By 1975 tensions between Palestinians (and their Sunni and Druze backers) on the one side and the various Christian militias on the other had reached fever pitch. Israel and America armed the Christian militias, and Syria in large part supplied the Palestinians.

The event that ignited the war took place on April 13, 1975, when a drive-by shooting in front of a church in East Beirut killed four congregants. The *Kata'ib* (Phalanges) militia, a working-class Maronite movement, struck back against the presumed culprits. Its members attacked a bus carrying twenty-seven Palestinians, killing the riders inside. The army soon disintegrated into sectarian camps, and the civil war began.

By November 1975 the Kata'ib moved into downtown and West Beirut—the Sunni Muslim side of town—overtaking several hotels, including the iconic Holiday Inn Tower in the seaside neighborhood of Ayn al-Mreisseh. A coalition of Muslim groups, going by the name of the National Movement, reprised by taking the nearby Murr Tower, from which they launched an attack of heavy machine guns and rocket launchers on the luxury hotels. The onslaught destroyed "bastions of the moneyed elite whose roots ran back to the creation of Greater Lebanon."[7] To this day, the Holiday Inn remains in its place, an empty shell serving as yet another reminder of what a country can do to itself.

The fighting soon escalated. By December of that year, the brutality of sectarian conflict had reached new heights. Four Christians were found shot in a car in East Beirut, and in reprisal Bashir Gemayel, son of Pierre and heir to his father's mantle of leadership, ordered an attack on the first forty Muslims the Kata'ib could find. It wasn't long before the victims arrived at a checkpoint on the Christian side of town, "some of them traveling with their wives and children in their family cars to homes in East Beirut." Members of these unsuspecting families were taken away at once to have their throats slashed.[8]

The factions fought, not only on sectarian grounds, but as groups led by particular leaders seeking total obedience. In 1977 Bashir Gemayel ordered the murder of Tony Franjieh, the son of Suleiman Franjieh, erstwhile competitor of the Gemayels. To make a point, the Kata'ib "first forced Tony and his young wife to watch the shooting of their baby. Then the gunmen made Tony Franjieh witness the murder of his wife."[9] Finally, it was Tony's turn. No one, not even a fellow Maronite, was immune from the brutality of the Kata'ib.

The Sabra and Shatila massacre stands as one of the ultimate examples of callous and unrelenting brutality in sectarian war. On the heels of the assassination of Bashir Gemayel on September 14, 1982, the Lebanese Forces (LF), the umbrella party to which the Kata'ib belonged, decided to retaliate hard against the Palestinians. The Sabra and Shatila refugee camps had been cleared of most fighters after Yasser Arafat had agreed to disarmament and departure from Lebanon. Only the most frail and defenseless, the elderly, the women, and the children, had been allowed to remain in the country as part of the agreement. On the night of September 16, 1982, vengeful Christian militiamen crept into the camps and began a slaughter that would not end until the morning of September 18.

The killings possibly numbered in the thousands[10], though no one will ever know exactly how many perished during the span of one and a half days. What went through the minds of LF members as they slay their defenseless victims is impossible to know. But fear, unrelenting, unmanageable fear of "the other"—the other sect, the other faction, the other leader—is what runs deep in the veins of every sectarian fighter. It lies beneath the surface, beneath crowded layers of consciousness. At the heart of every atrocity is a fear, rational or otherwise, that perceives the world as a contest for survival: "It is either them or me."

The Sabra and Shatila massacre could easily have come from the annals of ancient history, but it was 1982 that saw a U.S.-backed militia carrying out a communal death sentence while Israeli soldiers, who had entered Lebanon to route out Palestinian terrorists, simply gazed from adjacent rooftops. Giving a firsthand account of the scene of the war crime, Robert Fisk describes "women lying in houses with their skirts torn up to their waists and their legs wide apart, children with their throats cut, rows of young men shot in the back after being lined up at an execution wall. There were babies ... tossed into rubbish heaps alongside discarded US army ration tins, Israeli army medical equipment and empty bottles of whisky."[11] The massacre, vengeance for the killing of Bashir Gemayel, had been targeted at the wrong community: Gemayel, it turned out, had been killed by a fellow Christian.

Israel, which had entered the fray in the spirit of self-defense, could not help but be pulled into the killing in the Lebanese civil war. Like other modern Western armies, Israel's involvement in the war was largely absent the point-blank murders and the throat slashings, but it wasn't any less brutal. In August 1982, before the Israeli Defense Forces (IDF) sat by and watched the systematic rape and murder of countless unarmed

Palestinians, it did some heavy killing of its own. After the repeated pounding of Beirut from the air had proved only moderately successful in routing the Palestinian militants, Israel launched a relentless, saturation bombing campaign on August 12. This airborne conflagration over once-chic Beirut came to be known as Black Thursday. The event left over five hundred civilians dead and countless displaced, and brought widespread disease and infestation in the absence of running water and food supplies. An outside sectarian feud, the one between the Israelis and the Palestinians, was now being fought to the death on Lebanese soil.

With the bombing, Israel won the battle. The PLO could no longer put the Lebanese through untold carnage, and its forces retreated to their new headquarters in Tunisia and to countries across the Middle East. When the men were gone, the Sabra and Shatila massacre took place, and Israeli soldiers, with the acquiescence of their leadership, watched it all take place.

Ariel Sharon, then-minister of defense, was eventually held "indirectly responsible" for the bloodletting at Sabra and Shatila. When he made a comeback as Israeli prime minister in 2001, in the midst of the second Palestinian uprising, or *Intifada*, Palestinian hatred for the man was insurmountable. Many American onlookers didn't understand why Sharon, whom President George W. Bush referred to as a "man of peace," was so profoundly hated. But if America had forgotten Sabra and Shatila, the Palestinians had not.

Given its bitter success in routing out the PLO, Israel would attempt a similar operation again. As a response to the incursion of Hezbollah fighters into Israeli territory in 2006, which led to the killing of five Israeli soldiers, the Jewish state launched a bombing campaign over much of Lebanon, including the airport and key infrastructure. Israel thought it could defeat Hezbollah, as it had the PLO. But it miscalculated. Although Hezbollah was created with the help of Iranian agents, it was a homegrown movement, and this set it apart from the PLO. Hezbollah was, and still is, as Lebanese as the cedars of Mount Lebanon. The PLO may have been compelled to leave Lebanon in 1982 after the Israelis' massive bombing campaign, but Hezbollah in 2006 had nowhere else to go.

From the outset, then, it should have been obvious that a political movement of Hezbollah's sort—characterized by militia members stashing weapons under their mattresses and women preaching the message of resistance to their children—could hardly be rooted out through aerial bombing alone. The thirty-three days of air strikes only emboldened Hezbollah and unraveled the image of Israel as an invincible military power.

Today, the Muslim street considers the July 2006 War as the first-ever victory by an Arab army against Israel, and this has earned Hezbollah a kind of mythical status across sectarian lines. This was not just because Hezbollah didn't succumb to Israeli pressure, but because it had the weapons to fight back.

Every night of the conflict, Iranian-made missiles rained down on northern Israel, while Hasan Nasrallah preached perseverance on the Hezbollah-run Al-Manar television. The Arab populations, having suffered the indignities of repeated military defeats at Israel's hand, were collectively praising the Iranian-funded Shia of South Lebanon, all while their frightened leaders planned the next move against a resurgent Iran and the growing "fifth column" of Shias in the Arab world.

Today, Lebanon is still fractured along sectarian lines. In Beirut, Sunnis mostly live in the west, Christians in the east, and Shias in the south, with the Druze dwelling in small pockets throughout the city. Yet the balance of power has shifted significantly in the Shias' favor. For one, the Shia are largely united under the banner of Hezbollah, an organization that is part militia, part revolutionary social movement, part political party, and part country.

Hezbollah operates with complete autonomy in the Shia areas of South Lebanon and South Beirut, and it commands a military force that is significantly stronger and more cohesive than anything the Lebanese army and the other sectarian factions put together can currently muster. Politically, Hezbollah also benefits from the divisions within the other sects. While Sunnis have been historically reluctant to get dragged into a fight with the Shia, Christians are divided between those who are willing to work with Hezbollah, and a minority that looks forward to renewed fighting. The Druze are split along similar lines.

In May 2008, following a months-long political impasse over the selection of a president, Hezbollah's army made a brief military incursion into Sunni West Beirut, an exercise that left sixty-two people dead. Sunnis, an increasingly elite group inside Lebanon, could do little to stop it. The political gridlock ended, Hezbollah pulled back and declared a victory.

Despite the violence, it may surprise many Westerners to learn that those looking to fight Hezbollah are considered extremists inside Lebanon, if anything because the Iranian-backed group is so powerful that openly opposing it can border on suicidal. The balance of power has come to favor Hezbollah after 2006, but that could always change in the blink of an eye.

In the summer of 2008 the forces of polarization were once again on the prowl. In northern Lebanon, Syrian-backed Alawites (of the unique brand of Shiism associated with the Syrian regime) were engaged in pitched battles with Salafi Sunnis—presumably armed and funded by Saudi Arabia. That Saad Hariri, son of late prime minister Rafik Hariri, was born in Saudi Arabia and held Saudi citizenship, made the connection all the more obvious to his critics in Lebanon. His father, after all, had been killed by the Syrian-Alawite government. Religious polarization in the name of geopolitical jostling is unlikely to go away any time soon.

8

CHAOS AND PROMISE

Operation Iraqi Freedom began on March 20, 2003. In the first seventy-two hours of the campaign, more than 2,500 munitions were dropped on Iraq, while the I Marine Expeditionary Force and the Army V Corps engaged in a series of battles against Iraqi regular and Republican Guards forces, dealing an irreversible blow to the Iraqi state. Despite some setbacks for the U.S. military, Baghdad fell on April 9 of that year, bringing to an end the twenty-four-year rule of Saddam Hussein.[1]

The historic military victory of U.S. forces was short-lived. Soon after the fighting stopped, the looting began. Men, women, and children took part in the rampage, a destructive sandstorm that broke through the gates of a once-sturdy fortress. Even the National Museum in Baghdad was looted, resulting in the theft and destruction of thousands of artifacts dating back to Iraq's beginnings, the start of civilization itself. The director of the British Museum called it at the time "the greatest catastrophe to afflict any major institution since the Second World War."[2] Because of the overnight collapse of state cohesion, Iraq disintegrated into lawlessness and random violence. Thomas E. Ricks aptly writes that because "the Pentagon assumed that U.S. troops would be greeted as liberators and that an Iraqi government would be stood up quickly, it didn't plan seriously for less rosy scenarios."[3]

As soon as Saddam's regime fell, a predictable cast of characters emerged to take control of postwar Iraq. On the newly strengthened Shia front was Ayatollah Muhammad Baqir al-Hakim and SCIRI, fresh out of exile in Iran. After al-Hakim was killed, his brother Abdul Aziz took over the SCIRI, which was later renamed as the more mild-sounding Supreme Islamic Iraqi Council (SIIC).

The other Shia faction with national reach was the *Jaish al-Mahdi*, or Army of the Messiah, founded by Muqtada al-Sadr in the summer of 2003. More commonly known in English as the Mahdi Army, the militia's members totaled sixty thousand in 2007, though it is not clear how many of them constitute a cohesive force today. Once the largest coherent military power in Iraq after the United States, the Mahdi Army fought some of the fiercest battles by any Shia group against both American forces and the Badr Organization, the armed wing of the Iranian-backed SCIRI. Today, however, what is left of the Mahdi Army is increasingly falling under Iran's grasp, and away from Muqtada.

On the Sunni front, the initial bulk of the anti-American insurgency comprised disaffected Baathists leftover from Saddam's regime. These were largely bureaucrats and former military and intelligence officers who were given little reason to embrace the new Shia-friendly order. It didn't help that L. Paul Bremer III, the American viceroy between May 2003 and June 2004, called for the general "de-Baathification" of the military and governing class. In May 2003 Bremer issued two of the now infamous Coalition Provisional Authority (CPA) orders: one that "banned persons serving in the top four levels of the Ba'ath Party from holding government employment" and another that "dissolved Iraq's army, its air force, its navy, its secret police, its intelligence services, the Republican Guards, the Ba'ath Party militia, and the Ministry of Defense."[4] This affected a total of thirty thousand civil service workers who were by far the best equipped to run the country during a time of crisis.[5]

Despite the noble political intentions of de-Baathification, American planners didn't seem to think about the potential consequences that such disaffection would inspire among the government elites. Those who defend American decision making during the reconstruction will say that the military, for one, had already disbanded on its own by the time U.S. tanks rolled into Baghdad. But while this was largely true, it is hard to make the case that an olive branch, calling for the immediate restitution of salaries and a general pardon for crimes committed, might not have inspired at least some cooperation from those whose job and life had been centered around running the country (and who would eventually join the insurgency in staggering numbers).

Another Sunni faction, however, cared little for the former Baath Party, as it was mostly led by foreigners. Al-Qaeda in Mesopotamia was started by Jordanian-born Abu Musab al-Zarqawi, who quickly became the most notorious terrorist inside Iraq. With the Iraqi landscape teeming with American military personnel, Salafi recruits arrived in staggering numbers from neighboring Sunni countries, armed with a hatred for Shiism that rivaled even their anti-Americanism. One study by the U.S. Military Academy's Combating Terrorism Center showed that up to 75 percent of suicide bombers in Iraq between August 2006 and August 2007 were foreigners.[6] These Wahhabis would go on spectacular missions against crowded Shia markets, mosques, restaurants, and other soft targets, and thereby helped the sectarian war reach a higher level of carnage. As the war raged on, nearly 2.5 million Iraqis were displaced, with thousands of sectarian killings reported each month during its peak.

Strategically, al-Qaeda wanted to establish a base of operations in the Middle East that could recruit fighters by taking up the banner of resistance to foreign occupation. Neighboring Sunni countries, if not complicit, did not do enough to turn off the spigot of willing suicide terrorists, who used their territory as transit points, and who often hailed from particular cities within given Sunni countries—a fact that betrayed the stable presence and operation of al-Qaeda recruiting networks. By 2006, around 60 percent of all foreign fighters had come into Iraq from Saudi Arabia and Libya.[7] Even if recruits didn't flow freely in many U.S.-allied states, anti-American propaganda certainly did. On Egyptian television, the al-Zawra satellite channel featured the glorified images of American convoys being blasted by Sunni insurgents, yet it was kept on the air until 2007.[8]

The sectarian edge of the violence was felt early on, but it only worsened as the months went on. Muhammad Baqir, the elder Hakim, was assassinated in August 2003, falling victim to a car bomb detonated outside the Imam Ali Mosque in Najaf (Ali's resting place). The explosion killed a total of 124 people.[9] Some believed the bombing had been ordered by Shia rival Muqtada al-Sadr, while al-Hakim's faction officially pointed the finger at Baathist insurgents. Today, al-Zarqawi's jihadist network is believed to have been behind the attacks. The American military suspected this early on, as the attack was consistent with al-Qaeda's systematic efforts to generate divisions inside Iraq and thus create an environment of sectarian chaos suitable for its survival and expansion.

The United States had entered Iraq under the assumption that it could restore stability by arming and training a new Iraqi security force. But as the United States struggled to train and field enough Iraqi troops to even marginally quell the violence, these very forces were at once targeted by al-Qaeda and Sunni insurgents, sometimes as they stood in line to apply for the dangerous job. Making matters worse, those who did join were often tied to other interests, particularly the rival Shia militias that formed the backbone of the emerging Iraqi regime. Ricks quotes Army Command Sergeant Major Michael Clemens saying: "[Iraqi soldiers] tend to react to things as Shia first and as soldiers second. We had to remind them that they're an apolitical organization and they couldn't drive around in their Humvees with pictures of Moqtada al-Sadr plastered on the back and their green Shia flags."[10]

Bent on settling old scores with the Sunnis, the Shia militias would use their official positions inside the government to obtain weapons and provide cover for sectarian cleansing campaigns. In fact, much of the Mahdi Army's arsenal of rocket-propelled grenades and improvised explosive devices was taken directly from the weapons caches of the Iraqi security forces.[11]

One of the underreported blunders of the war was the concurrent attempt by the United States to fight a Sunni insurgency while engaging in escalating rhetoric with Tehran over its nuclear program. Given the undeniable historic connection between Iran and the majority Shia of

Iraq and given the legacy of the Iran-Iraq War, Iran had a greater stake in the future of Iraq than America ever would. To expect Iran to either disengage from Iraq altogether or make life easy for U.S. troops there while America threatened its regime's survival over its nuclear program was shockingly misguided. It will never be known how many U.S. and Iraqi lives might have been saved had the United States attempted to foster closer coordination with the top echelons of Iranian intelligence from the outset of the invasion. To put it differently, if America wanted to make its opposition to Iran's nuclear program a centerpiece of its foreign policy, it should have never invaded Iraq.

The greatest missed opportunity for collaboration between Tehran and Washington came on the eve of the invasion, when the Iranian government sent a secret fax to the White House, offering "to talk about everything from its controversial nuclear program to support for Hizbullah and Hamas." The Bush administration must have been overcome with a feeling of sheer invincibility because the president was in no mood to negotiate. The United States not only ignored the historic overtures but also "scolded the Swiss ambassador in Tehran at the time for passing the message on."[12]

The Islamic Republic had a stake in stabilizing Iraq, but regime survival and national security took top priority. Soon Iran was investing in its prior foes, notably the nationalist Muqtada al-Sadr, who began receiving weapons and training from Iran's elite Qods, or "Jerusalem" Force, perhaps as early as the summer of 2003. It was then that Muqtada went to Iran to pay a visit to his ideological mentor and exiled Iraqi ayatollah, Kazem al-Haeri, along with Qods commander Qassem Suleymani. With Muqtada moving closer to the Islamic Republic, a proxy war seemed to be unfolding in Iraq between the United States and Iran, two countries that had started out with the same goals in mind: the end of the Baath regime, the defeat of anti-Shia, al-Qaeda-like forces in Iraq, and a democratic (in this case meaning Shia-led) government in Iraq.

At the heart of the many blunders, however, was the invasion itself. It was blind conviction on the part of U.S. policymakers that led them to the idea that American democracy and political values could be transplanted anywhere, anytime, and under the most unwelcoming of circum-stances. To this day proponents of the war speak of "liberating" Iraq, as if Saddam had been some alien force in his own country. The Allies liber-ated France in 1943 but America and Britain invaded and occupied Iraq in 2003, and the difference between liberation and occupation could not be greater in the eyes of the local population. Ali A. Allawi, cousin of Iraq's interim prime minister, writes,

> Soon after arriving in Baghdad, [Bremer] started to give TV addresses to the Iraqi public, explaining his policies and hopes for the future. Very few Iraqis could relate to what he was try-ing to convey. The US slogans and catch phrases of his media advisers did not resonate with his public. Words such as 'lib-erty' and 'freedom' translated poorly into the customary politi-cal usage of most Iraqis, and did not carry the same meaning or significance in Arabic. ... Unfortunately, the CPA insisted on forcing its own image of what Iraq was or should be, and but-tressing its representations by copious reference to polls and focus groups.[13]

For the U.S. administration, elections and de-Baathification were prerequisites for a new Iraq. How otherwise would the American public, which had grown up scorning the Axis powers' invading armies of World War II, be made to stomach the unprovoked attack and occupation of a sovereign state? If talk of weapons of mass destruction sold the war to the American public, championing U.S. democracy would make the end result much more palatable and remove any potential stain that might be incurred from invading a country that had neither attacked nor realisti-cally had the power to inflict pain upon America.

But while de-Baathification and a quick move toward free elections, which came on January 30, 2005, made sense from the vantage point of American public opinion, they did not necessarily bode well for the future of Iraq. Most presciently, Jack Snyder warned back in 2000 against na-ively "pressuring ethnically divided authoritarian states to hold instant elections."[14] While Iraqi Sunni and Shia Arabs do not represent different ethnic groups, their sociopolitical narratives have been constantly at odds in the country, and their political experience as Iraqi communities are different enough to generate adversarial impulses such as those we have witnessed in the sectarian civil war.

Snyder could have been referring to Iraq when he wrote, "Effective institutions for channeling social cleavages in other directions need to be well developed before democratization can be part of the solution rather than part of the problem."[15] Certainly, Iraq qualifies for Snyder's apt descriptions of postcolonial states that are fed on the patronage of one group over another, and in which "factionalism in politics during their democratization often follows ethnic lines."[16] If you are a Shia in postwar Iraq, you will vote with your coreligionists, while Sunnis will do the same. If you are a Kurd, you will vote for a Kurdish party. This isn't an expression of blind discrimination or even a lack of idealism, but instead it is a reflection of national realities, that is, the pattern of mutual antagonism that was written into Iraq's DNA when it was created in 1920.

Of course, this faith in democracy as the cure-all has been part of the American tradition. Who, after all, would not want everyone to live in freedom? The problem comes when two important preconditions for democracy, security and a common national narrative, are simply absent in the country one is trying to democratize. Because postwar Iraq became an anarchic state teeming with acerbic sectarianism, and because it lacked even the faintest tradition of democracy, voting became little more than an avenue for the expression of sectarianism. As Samuel P. Huntington bemoaned in his groundbreaking 1968 work, *Political Order in Changing Societies*, "When an American thinks about the problem of government-building, he directs himself not to the creation of authority and the accumulation of power but rather to the limitation of authority and the division of power ... His general formula is that governments should be based on free and fair elections."[17] It may be called a miracle if such a formula survives much longer in Iraq.

So what happens when democracy is insisted on? In the 2005 parliamentary elections, Islamist Shia and Kurdish blocs earned nearly 63 percent of the seats.[18] As was the case in Lebanon, the outcome of elections becomes an issue not of who has the most persuasive ideas but rather of which sectarian group has the most members. In many ways, however, Iraq's situation is far less promising than that of Lebanon, where the National Pact has at least allowed the sects to maintain some degree of power sharing. For Iraqi Sunni Arabs, however, being a minority in an open democracy is a dire predicament that could lead to political oblivion—by far a worse outcome for them than perpetual civil war.

As the insurgency gained strength, the Bush administration could do little to ignore it. It would eventually have to fight it. The wake-up call did not come from Baathist insurgents, but from al-Qaeda. On February 22, 2006, a set of bombs was exploded inside the Grand Mosque in Samarra, plummeting the structure's iconic golden dome and destroying much of the building in the blasts. The incident led to "retaliatory attacks against 60 Sunni mosques and the killing of more than 400 Sunnis by Shi'a militias in the bombing's immediate aftermath."[19] Soon, entire neighborhoods were cleansed, with the Iraqi security forces often acting as a front for the brutal Shia militias of al-Hakim, al-Sadr, and their uncontrollable associates. The Sunni Baathists fought back, and al-Qaeda was happy to continue its attacks on critical infrastructure and soft targets.

The Contenders for Power

The three catalysts of sectarian conflict are alive and well in Iraq today. First, there are various factions, led by individual leaders and families bent on maximizing their share of power at the expense of just about everything and everyone else. Second, there is a lack of cohesive state authority, despite the success of the 2007 U.S. troops surge. Last, the power struggle between forces of "eastern" Iran, and the "western" parts of the region, in this case the Sunni Arab regimes, has reemerged in Iraq, keeping alive a colossal battle that may never be won, but which will likely always be waged.

In the invasion's aftermath, a set of groups came to play major roles in defining the Iraqi civil war, namely, the major Shia and Sunni organizations, as well as the ever-present Iranian agents. An overview of each follows.

The Badr Organization

The Badr Organization, originally the Badr Brigade, is the military arm of SCIRI, which Iran created in 1982 (the same year it helped establish the Lebanese Hezbollah). Both Hezbollah and Badr have officially embraced Khomeini's philosophy of wilayat al-faqih, though in 2007 SCIRI softened its image by aligning more closely with Ayatollah Sistani and changing its name to the Supreme Islamic Iraqi Council.

Badr fought alongside Iranian forces during the Iran-Iraq War, functioning as a unit of the Qods Force—the elite foreign operations arm of Iran's Revolutionary Guard. Throughout the 1990s, Iran's support of opposition groups in Iraq was consistent with its policy of regime change vis-à-vis Saddam Hussein, and Iran is known to have earmarked around $20 million in aid per year to the Badr Brigade throughout the decade.[20]

After the 2003 invasion Badr became one of the most important sources of political muscle behind the emergent, Shia-led government in Iraq, though it was soon dwarfed in size by the Mahdi Army. (Badr started out in 2003 with around fifteen thousand fighters, though as a force it has largely been incorporated into the Iraqi military and intelligence services. In comparison, the Mahdi Army peaked at around sixty thousand members in 2007.)

During the height of sectarian violence, Badr members were known to engage in bloody, anti-Sunni missions while donning official government garb. In particular, the Badr, like the Mahdi Army, has been charged with using local death squads to cleanse entire neighborhoods of Sunnis, though it has also used its militias to protect Shia populations from Sunni insurgents and al-Qaeda suicide bombers.

On November 13, 2005, U.S. forces discovered a hush detention facility that was being reportedly run by the Interior Ministry, which was then controlled by SCIRI. In it, they found over 170 Sunni captives, who had been left starving. Some had been subjected to electric shocks or brutally beaten and had large swaths of skin missing. Such underground torture chambers had been talked about throughout Iraq, especially since it had become common for death squads to terrorize and drive away Sunni residents in Baghdad by dumping mutilated bodies on the street in broad daylight, most infamously bearing holes that had been carved with power drills.

To this day, many Iraqis view the Badr Organization and its parent SCIRI with suspicion and as proxy groups out to do Iran's bidding. When Muhammad Baqir al-Hakim returned to Iraq from exile in Iran in 2003, a spokesperson of rival Muqtada al-Sadr said that al-Hakim "represents outside forces and works with Iran, the U.S., and Israel. We need someone from inside who suffered with Iraqis and represents the people's voice. We don't want an Iranian state."[21]

Muqtada himself was more direct, blaming Iran for failing to support the 1991 Shia uprisings that were crushed in the aftermath of the Gulf War, and accusing al-Hakim of "betraying the people of Basra and the south when he urged them to fight and didn't help them, causing the [uprising] to fail."[22] This was the voice of the nationalist Shia of Iraq, led by the Sadrists.

The Sadrists

Muqtada al-Sadr's jump into the ring came just one day after the U.S. toppled Saddam Hussein's government. In a typical blood feud killing, Muqtada ordered the death of Majid al-Khoei, son of Grand Ayatollah Abu al-Qasem al-Khoei. Khoei had been engaged in a political battle with Muqtada's late uncle, Baqir, and the young al-Sadr found the postinvasion chaos a perfect opportunity to even a score. On April 10, 2003, al-Sadr's supporters allegedly dragged the young al-Khoei from the Imam Ali Shrine in Najaf and hacked him to death.[23]

Muqtada gained much of his street credibility as a member of the opposition who had stayed put in Iraq while his SCIRI rivals had worked out of Tehran. During Saddam's reign, Muqtada's long periods of suffering under constant fear of death became something of a brand for him, and even after the 2003 invasion he was known to wear a white funeral shroud during public speeches, giving him an aura of martyrdom in life.

Despite his honest indignation with Iran and his thorough nationalist credentials, Muqtada soon learned to accept favors from the Islamic Republic, a country that not only could help him, but also had the power to make life incredibly difficult for him. Muqtada began to form his Mahdi Army militia in mid-2003, but as early as April Ayatollah Haeri had already issued a fatwa from Qom naming Muqtada his "deputy and representative in all fatwa affairs. ... His position is my position."[24] This allowed Muqtada to borrow a level of religious legitimacy beyond his limited scholarly credentials at the time.

Not all followers of Muqtada's father, Sadiq al-Sadr, embraced Muqtada's emerging leadership with open arms. The Virtue Party (*al-Fadila*) was founded by Ayatollah Muhammad al-Yaqubi, a former student of Sadiq al-Sadr who split from the young Muqtada in 2003, in large part owing to his perceived inexperience, but also as a result of al-Fadila's more stringent anti-Iranian position.

Although al-Fadila is small, and it does not rise to the level of the Badr Organization or the Mahdi Army, Muqtada's forces did engage the party in a brief but pitched battle in Basra on March 22, 2007, the purpose of which was to oust al-Fadila's governor in the province, Muhammad al-Waeli. (The Mahdi Army failed that day, but the government of Prime Minister Nouri al-Maliki eventually succeeded in ousting Waeli on charges of oil smuggling in the spring of 2008.)

Like the Lebanese Hezbollah, the Mahdi Army provided key social services for the poor where it operated and had been keen to use the political process to its advantage, having had members appointed to lead several government ministries, including Health, Agriculture, and Transportation.[25] However, Muqtada's camp quit the governing party coalition in early 2007, all as part of a larger pattern of retreat that came with the 2007-08 U.S. troop surge. By 2008 the Mahdi Army's coherence was significantly diminished, particularly in the absence of its charismatic leader (Muqtada had left for Iran in 2006). In addition, Iraqi government crackdowns on Sadr City forced the organization to refrain from brandishing its firepower in public with the kind of impunity it had enjoyed before.

In the light of day, the Mahdi Army had been a vehicle for patriotic

Shia sentiment in postwar Iraq, though in the dark corners of the night, it had undertaken a brutal project of sectarian cleansing that will leave a lasting mark on the country. In Baghdad alone, the militia is thought to have been responsible for killing as many as thirty Sunnis per day during the height of the pre-surge sectarian war. One former Mahdi Army member explained, "It was very simple, we were ethnically cleansing. Anyone Sunni was guilty. If you were called Omar, Uthman, Zayed, Sufian or something like that, then you would be killed. These are Sunni names and they were killed according to identity."[26]

As of this writing, Muqtada is expected to return from Iran in late 2009, bearing his newly minted title of ayatollah, though such a move will ultimately be decided by Iran.

Sunni Insurgents

The term "Sunni insurgent" is broadly used to speak of disaffected Sunnis, many of whom held positions of influence during Saddam's regime. Although like al-Qaeda they are Sunni Arabs, their goals could not be more different from those of the jihadists. Based largely in the west and parts of northern Iraq, at any given time the insurgents may number from five to twenty thousand, and they go by names such as the Iraqi National Islamic Front, the Army of the Supporters of the Traditions, the Army of Muhammad, or the more extremist Army of Islam in Iraq. While their names and communications employ an Islamic tone, most Sunni insurgents hail from the secular elite of the previous regime. They are first and foremost Iraqi nationalists who have little patience for the concept of religious government, as advocated by al-Qaeda and its allies. The bad name garnered by the Baath Party over the years, however, has forced them to use the language of Islam as a recruiting and mobilization tool. (The "Islamization" of secular Baathists in Iraq is part of longer trend that started with Saddam's addition of the phrase *Allahu akbar* ["God is the greatest"] to the flag on the eve of the invasion of Kuwait in 1990.)

The driving goals of the insurgency have been, first, to avoid being shut out of the government by the rising tide of Shia majority rule, and second, bring about the end of the U.S. military presence as soon as possible. Needless to say, the early American policy of de-Baathification only helped strengthen the insurgency in its formative months, since it left experienced Sunni officers and bureaucrats with nowhere else to go. By 2006 up to "99 of 200 generals who served in the old Iraqi Army were probably active in the insurgency."[27] This figure speaks not only to the motives of the insurgency but also, just as important, to the talent and know-how the new Iraq lost in its transition to democracy.

Most Sunni insurgents make use of neighboring Syria as an operational safe haven, a trend that is owing in part to the lack of adequate border security in Iraq and to the 1.5 million Iraqi refugees who have crossed over into Syria since the conflict began.[28] Although the insurgents lack a unified structure, they are responsible for the vast majority of bombings in Iraq, as well as most attacks on U.S. military personnel. Most infamously, they have planted an untold number of roadside bombs (in the form of improvised explosive devises, or IEDs), which have inflicted the most casualties on, and severely hampered the mobility of, the U.S. military in Iraq.

Al-Qaeda in Mesopotamia

Since the invasion ended in 2003, Salafi fighters from Saudi Arabia, Libya, Yemen, Syria, Tunisia, Morocco, Algeria, Jordan, Egypt, and elsewhere have crossed into Iraq in alarming numbers (up to 10 percent of all al-Qaeda fighters are foreigners) to blow themselves up in crowded Shia marketplaces, at weddings, during pilgrimages, and in mosques.[29] According to the Brooking Institution's Iraq Index, over 61 percent of civilian bombing fatalities between January 2007 and January 2008 were a result of anti-Shia attacks; only 13 percent of such casualties resulted from anti-Sunni bombings.[30] At times, these suicide bombers have gone against harder targets, namely U.S. soldiers and Iraqi government officials.

Even though al-Qaeda in Mesopotamia is overwhelmingly made up of Iraqi volunteers, foreigners make up the higher rungs of the organization and to this day account for 80 percent of its suicide attacks.[31] By far the highest number of foreign al-Qaeda fighters are Saudi, followed by

Libyans, who often travel to Egypt before flying to Syria—the necessary stopping point for any Sunni militant wishing to fight in Iraq. The use of Syria as a transit point is critical, since it shows that even an ally of Iran can be fearful of the Islamic Republic's increasing power in the region, and actively work to undermine it.

A RAND Corporation study on counterinsurgency provides some detail about the goals of al-Qaeda recruits, stating that most "are not terrorists with global aspirations who would attack the United States if there were no war in Iraq. On the contrary, the are motivated primarily by the war."[32] This is not to say that al-Qaeda in Mesopotamia could not pose a long-term security threat once the United States left Iraq. In fact, there is a real possibility that al-Qaeda fighters could set up a permanent base in western Iraq if and when U.S. troops finally withdrew. This would be most problematic if Sunni insurgents and Sunni Arab governments provided a cushion for al-Qaeda to launch attacks against Iranian-backed Shias in Iraq, and potentially Iran proper, all in the name of minimizing the influence of the Islamic Republic.

Despite its relatively small size, al-Qaeda has had a disproportionate effect on the Iraqi conflict because it can stoke massive sectarian violence, as the bombing of the Golden Dome suggests. And following the official U.S. withdrawal from Iraqi city centers in July 2009, al-Qaeda has ramped up its violence against the usual soft Shia targets; that is, helpless civilians.

The Iranian Security Services

Aside from funneling arms and cash, and providing key military training to the Badr Organization and the Mahdi Army, along with some rogue Shia fighters, Iran has pushed its agenda by urging its "surrogates to assist US forces and position themselves to seize power through the electoral process."[33] This seemingly contradictory stance of undermining the American military presence while supporting Shia-favored democratic initiatives is a reflection of the equally schizophrenic policy that the Bush administration had pursued: It fought against al-Qaeda and Sunni insurgents, Iran's foremost adversaries in Iraq, while simultaneously making overt threats to Iran over its nuclear program. By arming rogue militias, Iran helped bog down U.S. military instruments, which may have otherwise been used to target the Islamic Republic.

For its part, Iran's supply of armor-piercing explosively formed penetrators (EFPs) to the so-called Special Groups—Shia fighters who split with Muqtada al-Sadr—led to a large number of U.S. casualties, reaching a high of 18 percent of U.S. and Iraqi troop fatalities in the last quarter of 2006.[34] These Special Groups are thought to be trained in camps near Tehran by Qods Force operatives and veterans of the Lebanese Hezbollah.

Yet Iran's involvement in Iraq is not purely military in nature. Apart from providing "electricity for many of the border towns,"[35] goods originating from Iran account for up to 50 percent of all imports into Kurdish Iraq. In addition, SCIRI-affiliated parties, bearing the names *Sayed al-Shuhada* (Master of the Martyrs), *Shaheed al-Mihrab* (Martyr of the Pulpit), and *Hizballah* (not to be confused with Lebanon's own), along with small local movements such as *Thar Allah* (God's Revenge), have been part of a wide network of Iranian-backed organizations that provide several layers of political insurance for Tehran, should one or many organizations buck under factional fighting or U.S. pressure. As a member of the Iraqi parliament once said, "America owns the sky of Iraq with their Apaches, but Iran owns the ground."[36]

Outside of the realm of the Mahdi Army and SCIRI political battles, some "extremist," or ghulat, organizations have emerged in Iraq. Reminiscent of early Islamic movements, these are led by fringe Shia-like charismatic leaders claiming to be the next messiah. Once such figure was Ahmad Hasan Yemeni, leader of the militant group *Jund al-Sama* (Soldiers of Heaven), whose members randomly opened fire on Shia worshipers during 2008 processions of Ashoura in Karbala. Jund al-Sama's previous leader, who thought of himself as the Hidden Imam al-Mahdi, had been killed one year prior after Iraqi security forces foiled an alleged plot to assassinate Ayatollah Sistani.[37]

Some Iraqis, however, suspect the government's apparent obsession with tiny Jund al-Sama is a pretext for arresting Shias who may never have been part of the group to begin with, but instead have been guilty of failing to express due loyalty to the SCIRI and its Iranian-affiliated groups. As if confirming its own insincerity, the Iraqi government has gone as far as to charge that the messianic cult is affiliated with al-Qaeda—the last organization that would be expected to align with a small, weak and very much fringe Shia group.[38] If the charges against the government are true, such an effort would be only part of a larger enterprise on the part of SCIRI to drive out Shias who reject Iranian meddling. As Muqtada al-Sadr quickly learned, having the second largest military entity in Iraq was not enough to effectively escape Iran's grasp.

The "Surge"

By March 2006 the Bush administration began to realize that a tactical shift was necessary; the war was going nowhere fast. Philip D. Zelikow, an aide to Secretary of State Condoleezza Rice, suggested a "massive effort to improve security in Baghdad" was needed in the form of additional troops.[39] Outside experts and even some members of Congress had been calling for a surge in troops, but for literally years the administration was restricted by its own reticence to accept the failure of former secretary of defense Donald Rumsfeld's light-weight approach to occupation.

With the massive loss of Republican congressional seats to the Democrats in the 2006 election, Donald Rumsfeld resigned. The new secretary of defense, Robert Gates, hailed from the George H. W. Bush administration, where he had served as CIA director. Part of a Washington club of realist policymakers, which included James Baker, Colin Powell, and George H. W. Bush, Gates "removed some of the institutional resistance at the Pentagon to the 'surge'" and brought renewed confidence in the civilian leadership.[40]

In January 2007, nearly four years after the start of the war, President Bush ordered five additional combat brigades to Iraq—nearly twenty thousand troops. Not merely a blind increase in troop strength, the surge was meant to hold neighborhoods in Baghdad and cities in the western Sunni province of al-Anbar for long enough to have newly trained Iraqi forces take over. Baghdad would be divided into nine administrative zones, with troops housed in forward-operating bases in the heart of the neighborhoods. The effects of the surge had been expected by November 2007, though significant drops in violence did not come until 2008.

In addition to military efforts at holding neighborhoods, which employed unmanned aerial drones for sophisticated seek-and-destroy missions, the surge was complemented by carefully planned political efforts on the ground. The most notable of these initiatives was the so-called Sunni Awakening, in which bands of former insurgents and al-Qaeda fighters, who either had enough with fighting or were enticed by American cash, stood down.

By 2008 the Awakening had become a force of between sixty-five and eighty thousand fighters, certainly strong enough to rival the Mahdi Army.[41] But it can hardly be expected that this force, which largely made a tactical decision to support America against al-Qaeda and now poses a threat to the central government in Iraq, will continue to remain helpful once U.S. payments stop flowing. In September 2008 al-Anbar was officially handed over to Iraqi security forces, though a residual force of twenty-five thousand U.S. troops was to remain.[42]

The *Army of Dude*, a blog written by Spc. Alex Horton, put it most bluntly, calling the Awakening "the ol' 'pay me more or I'm going back to killing you' ruse. . . . Commanders know that [the Sunni fighters] are important not for killing al-Qaeda, but for not fighting us. They're not allies, they're enemies with benefits."[43] Inherent in the Awakening strategy was the concern that strengthening the very forces that were antithetically opposed to the Iraqi government and the Shia rule they represented carried great risk for Iraq's long-term stability.

Shia political leader Sheikh Jalaluddin al-Saghir openly claimed that the "state cannot accept the Awakening. ... Their days are numbered."[44] Soon the Iraqi government began a crackdown against former al-Qaeda and Baathist insurgents who had been fighting jihadists in the western part of the country, a development that should have been seen coming from a mile away. By moving toward an equilibrium of Sunni and Shia forces, an explosive dilemma emerges. The more power is equally distributed, the less predictable the outcome of a potential war becomes, and hence the more likely groups are to take a chance in fighting.

As the Sunni Awakening took hold, the surge also benefited from Muqtada al-Sadr's tactical retreat. By doubling down on the fight against Muqtada in his stronghold of Sadr City, U.S. forces were able to push the radical Shia fighters toward a more accommodating position (in August 2007, Muqtada declared a six-month cease-fire). The vice around Muqtada soon became tighter, and in August 2008 an Iraqi court sentenced a senior leader of the Mahdi Army to death over the 2007 battle with the Badr Organization in Karbala, which had left fifty-two people dead.[45] And that same month, while the United States was negotiating a withdrawal from Iraq with the Shia government, Muqtada al-Sadr ordered his followers to halt violent activity completely and permanently.

Officially, Sadr's renunciation of violence, as well as his prolonged stay in Iran, was owing to his desire to reach ayatollah status by hitting the books in Qom. The one thing that kept Muqtada from being taken seriously by the likes of Sistani, after all, was his lack of Islamic credentials (he was a hujjatu al-Islam, and not an ayatollah). A hujjatu al-Islam is a rank achieved by a seminarian, but his words are not considered law, as those of a marja, or grand ayatollah, are. Muqtada's statements, then, carried mostly political and only limited religious weight. Those who followed the politics of Muqtada still had to choose, as pious Shias, which of the living marjas to emulate on religious matters. Hence, Muqtada al-Sadr's ability to lead without facing ridicule by his elders and political adversaries was limited.[46]

When Muqtada officially renounced violence in 2008 from his self-imposed exile in Iran, however, questions swirled around his true intentions for the cease-fire. In a statement, he declared, "Anyone who does not follow this order will not be considered a member of this group." As Vali Nasr has stated, the order to halt the violence might have been "face-saving talk," given the strategic blow dealt by the U.S. troop surge and Sadr's limited support from the Iraqi government and Iran. "He is the guest of the Iranian government who will control him," said Nasr, "until such time they have comfortably wrested control of the Mehdi Army away from him."[47]

Despite open calls for military calm, however, Muqtada's most ardent supporters answered by signing with their own blood an oath to keep fighting. "I prefer to resist by force using arms," claimed one of his supporters. "This is the only thing I am capable of doing."[48] As civil wars go, this may not be hyperbole. The longer the fighting, the harder it is to stop. In Lebanon, the most battled-hardened fighters found it most difficult to adjust to a peaceful life. Having grown up with fifteen years of war, they knew how to do little other than fight, and many are still waiting (or perhaps longing) for the next civil war.

But even with a temporary peace come another layer of dilemmas. If peace involves ceding the country to the majority Shia, can Sunnis be expected to accept this new reality without a fight? The U.S. troop surge, which resulted in some of the lowest levels of violence since the conflict began, has left many analysts with a dangerous level of optimism. But so long as the open question about the future course of Iraq, as a sectarian country in the middle of a dangerous region, is left unanswered, it is difficult to imagine a lasting stability, especially once U.S. troops fully withdraw and the real fighting for control of the country begins. So long as the three catalysts of sectarian conflict converge in Iraq, and the international community does not move adequately to understand them and mitigate their impact, there will likely only be more pain for the people of Iraq.

9

FUTURE OF A REGION

The Sunni-Shia conflict is a vexing phenomenon with many working parts to it. In fact, it is not a single conflict, but a tradition of jostling between massive states that have learned to leverage local religious culture for their own political goals. That said, certain basic ingredients are needed to allow countries to effectively make use of sectarianism. For one, a land in which the sectarian war is fought needs to be weak so that competing interests can be unencumbered by a functioning government. Second, individuals have to be motivated to action, their natural fears directed by powerful leaders who inspire a fierce loyalty among their followers.

In Iraq, where the United States has touched off a sectarian competition of massive proportions, the solution will not be found merely in adequate troop levels or efforts at intercommunal dialogue, though these are in fact important. What will matter most will be pursuing a policy that goes to the source of the sectarianism itself—the geopolitical rivalries that have been brought to bear on Iraq time and again.

For one, the U.S. invasion of Iraq shifted the balance of power in the Middle East in favor of Iran. This means that no matter how much Sunni Arab leaders may personally long for peace in Iraq, they will hardly be in a position to work toward the stability of a country that threatens their long-term interests. This is why it should not be surprising that suicide recruits from around the region have found their path to Iraq relatively unrestricted; and it only takes a few suicide bombings per month to keep Iraq from getting back on its feet and invite the kind of foreign capital and infrastructural development that would allow it to live up to its capabilities.

This is not to say that Sunni Arab countries are not concerned about the violence in Iraq, or for that matter than they are in complete control over what happens within their borders. It could very well be that they find themselves in a position of allowing Iraq to serve as a pressure release valve for homegrown Islamist movements. So long as an outside enemy such as Israel, and now the United States, is present in the region, governments can direct bad will and violent activity outwards, thus minimizing the threats to their own governments, all while conveniently sabotaging Iran's regional efforts.

What is certain is that most terrorists come from a handful of geographic locations, pointing to the relative ease with which jihadist networks operate in some countries. Joseph Felter and Brian Fishman of West Point's Combating Terrorism Center analyzed a sample of entries taken from al-Qaeda personnel records captured in Iraq.[1] They note that 60 percent of Libyan fighters came from the town of Darnah, a hotbed of Islamic extremism that has threatened Muhamar Qaddafi's reign in the past. Among Moroccans, 65 percent of the records sampled showed militants hailing from Casablanca, while 35 percent of Syrian fighters came from Dayr al-Zawr, from a province neighboring Iraq. Thirty-six percent of Algerians hailed from El Oued, a city of only about 140,000 inhabitants. Among all nationalities, a plurality of over 47 percent of suicide bombers found in those records were Saudis. Felter and Fishman write:

> As long as the Saudi government views foreign Sunni militants in Iraq as a bulwark against the dominance of Iranian-influenced Iraqi leaders, it is unlikely to invest heavily in stemming the flow of Saudis traveling to fight in Iraq. Limiting the real and perceived influence of Iran in Iraq's domestic political and

security situation may therefore be a necessary first step to gaining greater cooperation from Saudi authorities. A similar logic applies to gaining Syrian cooperation for interdicting or co-opting smuggling networks.[2]

It should be stressed that Syria's dominant role as a funnel for fighters, money and weapons into Iraq is a significant development in and of itself. Syria is one of Iran's few trusted allies, and it was among a handful that stood with the Islamic Republic during the Iran-Iraq War. The fact that Syria would turn itself into a launching pad for violent, anti-Shia and anti-government attacks in Iraq points to the scope of regional fears that a resurgent Iran inspires, even among current friends.

In one form or another, fears of Iran have existed in the Middle East ever since Iran became a global superpower in ancient times. Though the country has gone through periods of relative weakness over the last two and a half millennia, Iran's cultural autonomy, vast geography and strong sense of identity, have often generated perceptions of a sleeping giant. But the giant has awoken numerous times, in the form of a Sasanian Empire, a Safavid Dynasty, and more recently with the shah's U.S.-backed military buildup. Today, following the Iran-Iraq conflict, a war that proved that Iran could stand up against the will of both global superpowers, the United States and the Soviet Uinion, fears of Iran waking up should not be dismissed as hyperbole.

One question for the United States, of course, is whether increased Iranian power is necessarily unwanted. It is often taken for granted that America and Iran are natural enemies, when in fact the actions of both nations seem to point in the exact oppposite direction. George W. Bush rid the world of two of Iran's most dangerous adversaries, Saddam Hussein and the Taliban, the latter of which tried to instigate a war with Iran upon coming to power in Afghanistan in 1996. The Taliban then killed eleven Iranian diplomats, which prompted the Islamic Republic to amass troops along its border. Ever since, Iran instituted a policy of regime change, funding and arming the anti-Taliban Northern Alliance.

The United States has hundreds of thousands of troops in the region with the aim of maintaining pro-Iranian governments in place; governments that those in the rest of the region, including America's closest allies, are collectively hoping will fail. The United States is in a war against Sunni jihadists such as al-Qaeda and the Taliban, and not anti-Israeli terrorists like Hamas and the Palestinian Islamic Jihad, which Iran is funding. Hezbollah does have American blood on its hands, but its focus, unlike that of al-Qaeda, is purely regional and only marginally targeted at the United States (i.e., it has struck Americans only in its pursuit of larger regional goals, and not as an end in itself). In fact, Iranian support of these groups may be less important as America moves closer toward adopting a pro-Iranian position. The Islamic Republic has always supported these organizations as a means of avoiding the encirclement of other nations; it would just as well abandon them if it meant achieving greater security on its own terms.

All this said, it is not likely that America could move toward a pro-Iranian position too quickly without angering its current allies. After all, America brought the Sunni Arab governments "to the dance," so to speak, so not going home with them would do little to increase confidence in America's commitments to its friends. It may just be that the only way forward for the United States is to lessen the importance of places such as Iraq through a robust form of federalism. That is, ensure that Iran alone does not benefit from the U.S. invasion, but rather that other countries have a stake in its future. The last thing that America should do, however, is continue on its current path: act as if Iraq were an independent country that can somehow fight off foreign influence and remain pro-American and democratic. That is sadly a fantasy that is better abandoned sooner rather than later.

To begin negotiations on the future of Iraq, the United States could convene a series of summits aimed at finding a regional solution to the violence in Iraq; one that includes the active participation of Iran and the Arab world. Such summits would only be valuable inasmuch as the participants were willing to jettison formalities and empty declarations of their commitments to regional peace, and were instead willing to speak openly about their security and economic concerns. One critical topic would have to be oil: Together Iran and Iraq comprise some 18–20 percent of the world's proven oil reserves. Talk of a pro-Iranian, Shia dominated Iraq cannot take place without an honest accounting of concerns related to the distribution of energy resources.

In Iraq, a version of federalism that divides power among the Iraqi communities and leaves the Baghdad government as a coordinating, (rather than a governing) authority, may be an answer to the longterm security problems. In recent years, Iran has pushed exactly for such a degree of federalism, in essence seeking to annex parts of southern Iraq. The United States, which opposed any divisions of Iraq during the early years of the war, failed to foresee that at the end of the day federalism would be the lesser of the two evils. Today, we are faced with an Iraq that cannot realistically isolate itself from Iran. Federalism would merely contain the close friendship between the two countries to the Shia-dominated, southern portion of Iraq.

It goes without saying that such federalism would only work if Sunnis got at least some share of the oil. Between 70 and 80 percent of Iraq's oil reserves are found in the Shia south, but in the northern city of Kirkuk there are an estimated 20 percent of reserves, "all within commuting distance of downtown Kirkuk. Its fields, though half destroyed, still produce a million barrels of oil a day."[3] For any deal to work between the parties involved, Kirkuk, a city hotly disputed between Kurds, Turkomen and Sunni Arabs, would have to be handed over to the Sunnis, to be joined with a western Sunni region in a federalist Iraq. This region could in turn benefit from Sunni foreign capital, not unlike the way Iran currently aids Hezbollah-held areas of Lebanon. Sunni control over Kirkuk, with its potential to enrich Sunni Arabs and move them toward accepting the new, Iranian-dominated order in the rest of Iraq, will mean the difference between war and peace in the years and decades to come.

To be sure, a city such as Kirkuk cannot be simply "handed over," not when so many other factions are willing to fight for it. And as such, its oil cannot be simply pumped out through a pipeline and funneled to al-Anbar. This means that if the United States is committed to federalism, it will have to somehow convince the Kurds that Kirkuk is no longer theirs, a hard sell considering the pain that the community has suffered under Saddam Hussein, and its understandable anger over Saddam's forced "Arabization" of the city, which relocated large numbers of Arabs to the region in the first place.

Difficult as it may be to wrest Kirkuk from the Kurds and Turkomen, simply assuming that Sunnis in Iraq and across the region will accept an Iranian-dominated Iraq in which the Sunni community has no significant economic power is dangerously misguided. Something will have to give one way or another; the question is how large a war the international community is willing to stomach: a potential, localized war in Kirkuk, or a translational one over the whole of Iraq.

Regardless of what transpires, the United States and the international community have to abandon policies that are based on platitudes such as "democracy" and even "nation-building," vague terms that say little about the potential end-game. The sooner that international actors focus on power relationships, regional antagonism and alliance maintenance, the sooner the world can begin speaking about a peaceful, or at the very least, less bloody, Iraq.

Amidst the sober analyses, however, there is an underlying reality that should be encouraging. The Sunni-Shia conflict is not, as some may argue, an intractable, eternal struggle between two ideologies. While religious language colors the conflict, it is in the political realm where the conflict is started and stopped. This means that regional diplomacy, a language that U.S. policymakers and politicians the world over can speak, can and will be part of the solution to the violence in Iraq, Lebanon, and the rest of the region.

The Sunni-Shia conflict began in Iraq in the year AD 656, with the first Muslim civil war. In it, the Partisans of Ali, the progenitors of the Shia, fought the armies of the Party of Uthman, which later helped form the Umayyad dynasty and officially shut out the Shia from the government of the Islamic state.

Islam was shaped by these political intrigues, many of which took the form of one religious faction dueling against another within a state that was too large for even the most capable administrators to keep under control. Leading these factions were charismatic leaders, some of whom claimed divinity, while others counseled a return to Islamic puritanism. This factionalism ultimately fed the ambitious plans of emerging empires, which were quick to put various theologies to use as their official state instruments of propaganda. In most of the region, but particularly in Mesopotamia, the three catalysts of sectarian conflict—charismatic leaders, the breakdown of state power, and geopolitical battles—have converged to disrupt any movement toward internal peace.

Back in the ninth century, power vacuums were filled by competing claims in Baghdad and throughout Muslim lands, but soon enough the traditional geographic power centers in the east and west, the kind dominant during periods of Roman-Iranian bipolarity, reemerged. The Sunni Ghaznavids and Shia Buyids were based in and around Iran and Iraq, while the Ismaili Shia Fatimids set up their empire in Egypt. By the eleventh century, the Seljuks had entered Iran and Iraq from Central Asia, via the mountains of inner Khorasan, and they soon adopted stringent Sunni ideals to counter the Fatimid missionary call throughout their domains.

In the thirteenth century, the Mongols invaded Iran and Iraq and set up their Il-Khanate in the east, while the remnants of what the Seljuks had built developed into the western Ayyubid and ultimately the Mamluk empires. These last two fought the Crusaders and Mongols on two fronts and gave birth to a puritanical Sunnism that cultivated a unique hatred for foreign interference in their lands. To this day, the ideas of the Mamluks' most powerful cleric, Ibn Taymiyya, influence the beliefs of Osama bin Laden and thousands of other jihadists.

Starting in the fourteenth century, the Ottoman Turks shook the world with their military prowess and ambition, becoming the most powerful state in the Islamic world, and along with that a venerable rival of Christian power in Southeastern and Central Europe. But back east, they were countered by the Safavids, a "Persianized" Turkish family that adopted the Shia faith as a counter to Ottoman Sunnism and a tool to recruit discontented former Ismailis who still lived in western lands. Soon enough, the Safavids had etched in stone the process, begun centuries prior, of tying Iranian nationalism with the Shia sect.

By the nineteenth century Middle Eastern power had all but fizzled. In this context, the three Ottoman provinces of Basra, Baghdad, and Mosul hosted a slew of competing tribal and sectarian influences, which the British only further divided with their invasion in 1914. By1920 the country of Iraq had been created as a European ploy against Turkish influence in the region. Yet despite British assurances, Iraq was not free until Britain finally left in 1932. Iraq, a country divided by ethnicity, tribe, and sect, was left to figure out its future amid chronic divisions, which only a ruthless Baath Party was able to tamp down in earnest.

By the mid-1990s Iraq lay weakened under heavy sanctions and the legacy of two wars of expansion instigated by Saddam Hussein, as well as the horrific memories of the repression of Shia and Kurdish communities. But Iraq was contained. The United States had pursued a policy of dual containment that sought to keep both Iran and Iraq from exercising too much power in the Middle East, and it was working.

When the United States invaded Iraq on March 20, 2003, the country lay in the sights of Iran, just as it had for millennia. For most of history, Iran and Iraq have been intricately tied, initially not in terms of sectarian identity, but more so as a result of geography. Cyrus first invaded Babylon in 539 BC, and subsequent Iranian empires sought and largely succeeded in keeping parts of Mesopotamia under Iranian rule.

Today Iran continues to play a central role in Iraq. This fact comes to light when remembering that the most visible political leaders of postwar Iraq, from President Jalal Talabani to Prime Ministers Ibrahim al-Jafari and Nouri al-Malilki, from Muqtada al-Sadr to Abdul Aziz al-Hakim, have all at some point lived in Iran. The highest-ranking grand ayatollah in Iraq, Ali al-Sistani, is Iranian-born. Sistani's predecessor Grand Ayatollah Abu al-Qasem al-Khoei also hailed from Iran. Even the man who helped lead America to war in Iraq, the notorious Iraqi expatriate Ahmad Chalabi, has long-running ties to Iranian intelligence.[4]

Iraq's future will once again depend on the fight between Iran and its enemies, which today are the Sunni Arab governments of Saudi Arabia, Egypt and Jordan. The Sunni governments have thus far only tentatively helped Sunni insurgents, mainly by stoking fears of a "Shia crescent" and giving a voice to Sunni terrorists over the airwaves of Arab satellite television. Some funding, arms and suicide bombers have steadily entered Iraq from Sunni Arab countries, but not to the degree one would expect in an all-consuming, Lebanon-like civil war.

For its part, Iran has hedged its bets. During the Bush administration it helped democratic political process move along in Iraq, while at the same time arming some of the very militias that attacked and killed American troops, and tortured and killed large numbers of innocent Sunni civilians. In part, Iran sought to ensure a friendly Iraq while keeping American military instruments bogged down, lest they be turned against the Islamic Republic.

America's best hope will be to bring Iran and its Arab neighbors to the table and draw up a mutually agreeable course for Iraq's future. But this can happen only if the underlying struggle of regional power can be resolved. A grand bargain between Iran and the Arab nations is a difficult propostion, but it is the only viable option for achieving longterm stability. In the meantime, the Sunni-Shia conflict is likely to continue, not as an expression of theological disagreements, but as one of powerful regional interests, warring charismatic leaders, and a vacuum of state power that only the most brutal are able and willing to fill.

Companion Essay

ON HUMAN CONFLICT

> One knows from philosophical works the statement that
> 'man is political by nature.' ... The statement means that
> a single human being cannot live by himself, and his ex-
> istence can materialize only in association with his fellow
> men. ... Dealings with other people, when there is oneness
> of purpose, may lead to mutual affection, and when pur-
> poses differ, they may lead to strife and altercation. Thus,
> mutual dislike and mutual affection, friendship and hostil-
> ity, originate. This leads to war and peace among nations
> and tribes.
>
> —Ibn Khaldun, *Al-Muqaddimah* (1377)[1]

When most of us set out to make sense of a systematic chain of violent events, such as the genocide in Rwanda in 1994 or the Sunni-Shia cleansing campaigns of postwar Iraq, we are tasked with understanding the insensible. We might be tempted to ask whether one society or another is more prone to violence. Is the Rwanda genocide an "African" phenomenon? Are the problems in Iraq attributed to an "Arab mind-set" or violent impulses within the Muslim faith? Though many prejudiced observers throw around these questions in rhetorical fashion, many more of us, well meaning and curious, make similar inquiries in good faith. We want to understand why people are killing each other at such high rates, and what, if anything, we can do to stop the carnage.

When speaking to various audiences around the country on issues of U.S. policy in the Middle East, I've often been asked about the nature of the current civil war in Iraq: What are the religious differences between Sunni and Shia? What is the historical root of these disputes? This book provides answers to these questions, since having a grasp of the political and religious history of the Middle East is necessary to understanding the violence that mires the region. But just as important are questions that deal, not with the differences between Sunni and Shia per se, but with the simple calculus of power relationships that has always been at the heart of conflict.

More than understanding what makes Sunni and Shia fight, then, we need to understand what makes humans kill one another. This might sound like a curious philosophical exercise, but I assure you it isn't. Grasping the basics will be a necessary starting point if we are to avoid further mistakes and mischaracterizations about the origins of the Sunni-Shia conflict, or any other violent trend for that matter.

To be sure, killing on any scale is rarely moral or inherently just. Conflict might rear its ugly head while cloaked in questions of good versus evil, but that is rarely a consequence of objective reality. Because humans fight, they frame their fights in personal prejudices, in the form of right (*we*) versus wrong (*they*). But if we can put aside these natural, human prejudices for a moment and set out to discover the patterns of killing, raping, and pillaging in hotspots of the world; if we can view the genocide in Rwanda through the same lens as the genocide of the Native American peoples in what is now the United States, we might begin to understand some consistent patterns of group killing throughout history. This essay provides a framework for understanding conflict in general. If nothing else, it lays out as clearly as possible the philosophical and analytical perspective that I took when writing this book.

To start off, we should remember what leads people to war in the first place, something we seem to have forgotten as our country has become more powerful and we have entertained idealistic thoughts about our role in the world. Let's imagine, then, a simple, purely hypothetical scenario. We have two large groups—of people, animals, it doesn't matter. We'll call them Group A and Group B. If Group A desperately needs Group B's resources, and Group A is stronger than Group B (and there is no one else around to stop any potential aggression), what is likely to happen? What does our instinct tell us the answer to this question is? In fact, what is the easiest answer of all? Here it is: Group A will coerce, fight, and if necessary, kill, Group B. That is the simple answer to an eternally recurring question. We can comfortably assume, as theorists of war and peace have throughout the ages, that there is no need to psychoanalyze or mull over the religious preferences of Group A or Group B in order to predict an outcome. Destiny is written on the wall for all to see.

Today, such basic statements might read as controversial, but that is because we have forgotten those simple yet infinitely wise analytical approaches to policy formulation that have informed decision making from the dawn of man. Here, we are trying to relearn and rehash these "equations." We're trying to get back to the basics, so away with the coloring of right and wrong and of good versus evil. Let's keep it as A versus B, at least for now.

Notice that we are dealing with groups and not individuals. If A and B were individuals, we might expect different outcomes. If Individual A were to take pity on Individual B, we might not have a fight at all, just a quick glance before A would be on his way. That is to say that individual acts are more difficult to predict that group behavior. But why, then, is individuals less predictable than groups? Are groups not subject to the whims of selfish leaders, people like Adolf Hitler and Saddam Hussein? Are groups not larger versions of individuals? Not even close. The function of an organization is the welfare of the entire group. By this definition, the actions of a group are highly constrained. Because we have seen countries operate in more or less the same fashion throughout human history, we know there is little chance of a nation committing mass suicide or otherwise engaging in anything that can be called "unorthodox" behavior. Saddam Hussein's brutality and willingness to invade his neighbors was terrible. But unprecedented and unpredictable? Sadly, no.

When dealing with Middle Eastern nations, some pundits in the media often characterize heads of state as irrational actors: a macro version of suicide bombers martyring themselves for the cause of religion or the destruction of Israel. Some American commentators are quick to say that a nuclear-armed Iran will lead to the destruction of Israel (even though Israel sits on Muslim holy ground).[2] This faulty logic relies on the notion that Iranian leaders would be willing to commit national suicide to destroy a country that could strike back with its own nuclear weapons.

Yet if suicide bombers, the kind bankrolled by Iranian petrodollars in the West Bank, are suicidal, organizations aren't. The leaders of Hamas do not march into military checkpoints to blow themselves up. They hide. The suicide recruits are merely pawns (or soldiers, they would say) who give up their lives for the survival, and they hope, eventual victory, of their organization. Suicide bombers die willingly, but organizations want to live. Vicious? Yes. Irrational? Not for the organization.

In 2003 Robert Pape of the University of Chicago penned an article called "The Strategic Logic of Suicide Terrorism" (later published in book form).[3] His study looked at every recorded instance of suicide terrorism from 1980 to 2001, and found something chilling: suicide bombing tends to be used by organizations to gain territorial concessions, and the tactic has a tendency to work.

Looking at developments concerning Hamas in recent years, we get some anecdotal support for Pape's observations. That terrorist group's strategy had been to weaken the secular and increasingly moderate Palestine Liberation Organization (PLO), so that if and when Israel left Palestinian lands, Hamas would be poised to control them. Hamas made use of uncompromising language, calling for the total destruction of Israel, yet its leaders were too calculating not have realized they would never achieve such a feat. Instead, their attrition campaign targeting innocent Israeli civilians was carried out meticulously, starting in 1993, and it yielded significant results.

By waging a suicide bombing campaign, Hamas was able to paint itself as a legitimate resistance fighter—a label the more powerful (and corrupt) PLO had been unable to carry, particularly in the midst of dysfunctional peace negotiations with Israel. Hamas not only delivered many of the public services the PLO could not, but by engaging in suicide terrorism, it both signified a fighting stance versus the Jewish Goliath and disrupted the very peace process that would have given the PLO a moral victory. Every time a suicide bomb went off in Tel Aviv or Haifa, Israel was quick to retaliate against the PLO-held Palestinian Authority, which often had very little to do with the attacks but was too reticent to accept its own inability to stop them. By 2005 Israel withdrew from the Gaza Strip altogether—where Hamas' base of support lay—and by 2006 Hamas stood for parliamentary elections and handily won. Hamas' strategy of civilian killings was deplorable and barbaric, but was it irrational? Unfortunately, no.

Because an organization is tasked with the well-being of the entire group, its behavior is much more rational, and in many ways cautious, than any act by an individual may be. Organizations are constrained. A good way to think of the difference between group and individual behavior is to compare a solo pianist with a symphony orchestra. A pianist, while alone on the stage, can choose to interpret a Beethoven sonata in any way she sees fit. She may even ignore the notes penned by the composer and improvise on the spot. But such a sporadic, unplanned musical leap would be impossible for an orchestra to achieve without proper planning. In fact, real improvisation of any kind by a seventy-piece orchestra would automatically degenerate into noise.

An orchestra, as a group, is by definition restricted. It interprets music by the great composers through the voice of a conductor, who verbally expresses his or her wishes during rehearsals and who even keeps nonverbal tabs over the group of musicians with the baton during a performance. Even the nature of how the bow is used by the string sections is clarified ahead of time by a concertmaster. At the end of the day, an orchestra does nothing that is purely sporadic or uncontrolled. If it does, it is usually considered a mistake.

Group dynamics operate quite differently from individual action, if only because whims or raw feelings cannot be communicated to a mass of individuals and translated into seamless action. Even the most brutal dictators are beholden to a level of group self-preservation, and even group will. They are powerful, but not all powerful. No system of government is so efficient that it can transform a whim into perfectly coordinated action, not unless its execution is planned well ahead of time. And if it is, it has to make at least some marginal sense to those expected to carry it out.

Orchestra musicians might only roll their eyes if their conductor asks them to disrupt a traditional interpretation of Beethoven in favor of pure improvisation. But a nation marching toward self-destruction on the whim of an insane leader? This has occurred rarely in history, and only under the pretense that victory was at least possible, that there was some light at the end of the tunnel of insanity.

To be sure, the modern West is rarely on board with these basic readings of Groups A and B. Europe, enjoying a postwar security umbrella that has left it relatively free to engage in philosophical discussions on pacifism and collective security, hasn't been forced to deal with existential threats or the responsibility of steering the globe toward greater security. That has been America's job.

But if Europe has forgotten its "realist" past, America has been even more deceived by its post-Cold War power, which has erased any sense of vulnerability and, with it, many of history's hard-won truths. America has seen the threats and fought to avoid becoming a Group B of its own. In doing so, however, the United States has opened itself to the overzealous use of military force on a capricious hair trigger, increasingly draining its ability to buffer against the growth of competitive nations. As if power were a limitless resource, the United States has come to see itself as a group that can play by its own rules.

What historian Paul Kennedy calls "imperial overstretch"[4]—the military over-commitment that has brought down numerous superpowers throughout history—has now reached ominous proportions with the Iraq War. War planners stubbornly failed to see any limitations on American hard power, given that no other nation was strong enough to put a lid on U.S. ambitions in Iraq. Certainly, the more powerful a country becomes, the less it tends to be restricted by others and the more it is freed up to act in an ideologically motivated fashion. Ironically, while many U.S. policymakers vilify foreign tyrants as out of control and even suicidal in their lust for power, it is Americans, the unrestricted, who are at risk of turning into our own worst enemy. America is a Group A in a world of Group Bs, and it often tends to forget that.

In the run-up to the Iraq War, the Bush administration spoke of a clear and present danger, essentially scaring its country into a needless war. Iraq, President Bush said, gathered "the most serious dangers of our age in one place." It possessed so-called weapons of mass destruction, and it had "invaded and brutally occupied a small neighbor, has struck other nations without warning, and holds an unrelenting hostility toward the United States."[5]

At issue was Saddam Hussein's invasion of Iran in 1980 and Kuwait in 1990. What, other than sheer madness, many of us asked, could cause Saddam to invade two neighbors in the span of one decade? Unfortunately for the United States, there were very few clearheaded discussions about the potential pitfalls of an invasion in the media prior to the war. Instead, there was open psychoanalysis. "What we think of as crazy is normal for him," said Richard Perle in an interview in 2002 as chairman of the Defense Policy Board.[6] Saddam, Perle must have thought, was the crazy conductor of an orchestra who chose to play by his own tune.

Even Kenneth Pollack, a former CIA analyst who sat on the National Security Council during the Clinton administration (and who has otherwise been a sober analyst), implored Americans not to assume Saddam made decisions like a Westerner. Pollack particularly warned against "mirror imaging," a practice in which policymakers might ask, "What would I do if I were in his shoes?" For Pollack, who seemed to fetishize the "otherness" of the Middle East, it was certain that Saddam "does not think like an American president or even a Russian general secretary."[7] In other words, Saddam was loonier than the rest of us. And while that may or may not have been true, Pollack's assumption seems to have been that a leader's insanity automatically translates to insanity in action by the state. Those, needless to say, are two very different things (again, think orchestra versus solo pianist).

In suggesting that traditional forms of deterrence may not apply to Saddam Hussein, Pollack quoted Dr. Jerrold M. Post, a former CIA psychologist, who said that "Saddam's worldview is narrow and distorted and he has scant experience outside of the Arab world."[8] In an interview with the *Guardian* of London, Dr. Post, who frequently briefed senior U.S. policymakers in the run-up to the Iraq War, reached for what he thought was the heart of the problem: "It all goes back to his mother's womb. ... During the mother's pregnancy with Saddam Hussein, his father died, and another son died when he was only 12 years old. She both tried to commit suicide and to have an abortion."[9] European realists like Prince Metternich and Otto von Bismarck must have been turning in their graves—a war on advice of a shrink who had never met his patient.

Not to be outdone, Pollack goes on to provide his own conclusions about the Iraqi leader's mental state: "Saddam is determined to overturn the status quo to make himself the hegemon of the Persian Gulf region and the leader of the Arab world, to evict the United States from the region, and eventually to destroy the state of Israel."[10]

Some officials in the Bush administration went beyond psychoanalysis and engaged in open soothsaying. Condoleezza Rice, speaking to the BBC, said, "This is an evil man who, left to his own devices, will wreak havoc again on his own population, his neighbors and, if he gets weapons of mass destruction and the means to deliver them, all of us. It is a very powerful moral case for regime change."[11] The truth, apparently unseen by our civilian leaders at the time, was that timeless equations governing power relationships still applied to the modern Middle East. There were new threats, such as al-Qaeda, but there were no new states. That wheel had never been reinvented, and Iraq was not that special.

Once Saddam had been ousted from Kuwait in 1991 and his power restricted through crippling sanctions and the constant patrol of U.S. and British jets over UN-mandated no-fly zones, Iraq was no longer a threat to its neighbors. Its military spending went "from over \$15 billion in 1989 to less than \$1.4 billion a year through the 1990s."[12] The world community had significantly restricted Saddam's power, but who was going to restrict America's?

The 2003 invasion took place because the United States under George W. Bush assumed that any country might act on impulse. The difference between America and prewar Iraq, however, was that the United States was not restricted in its options, and Iraq was.

But what of Saddam's previous aggressions? Were they not the acts of an insane leader? Not exactly. In both 1980 and 1990, Saddam Hussein had seen an opening for expanding his nation's influence and jumped at the opportunity. The 1978–79 Iranian Revolution had thrown Iraq's neighbor into severe internal turmoil, and Saddam viewed this as an opportunity to act on irredentist claims over the oil-rich Shatt al-Arab region, on the border between Iran and Iraq. While Iran was engaged in a postrevolutionary struggle for power, Saddam invaded, touching off an eight-year war that turned out to be among the bloodiest in modern history. That Arab countries like Saudi Arabia, Egypt, Jordan and Kuwait, along with both the United States and the Soviet Union, sided with Iraq should say much about Saddam's confidence that he had made the right decision.

Fast forward to 1990. The Soviet Union was crumbling, and its former satellites and republics began to go their independent ways. The world map was being redrawn at breakneck pace, and again, Saddam knew this was his time to act. His dispute with the Kuwaiti royal family lay with the latter's circumvention of Organization of Petroleum Exporting Countries (OPEC) quotas (i.e., Kuwait was exporting more oil than it was supposed to), along with accusations that Kuwait was slant drilling across the border into Iraqi oil reserves. This, in addition to several billions of dollars that Iraq owed Kuwait for its assistance during the Iran-Iraq War (which Iraq, of course, did not want to pay), made Saddam determined to take over the much smaller country. Kuwait, after all, had been claimed by Iraq since 1920. And Saddam realized that, like Iran, Kuwait was swimming in oil. It was the classic game of Group A going after Group B's resources.

But before he could unleash his then-powerful military instruments, Saddam had to gauge how the United States might respond. According to a controversial transcript published in the *New York Times*, a meeting took place on July 25, 1990, between April Glaspie, U.S. ambassador to Iraq, and Saddam Hussein. From that meeting, Saddam seemed to come away with the message that America would not intervene should he invade Kuwait. Glaspie purportedly told Saddam that America had "no opinion on the Arab-Arab conflicts."[13]

It should be noted that some have disputed the authenticity of the report, as well as its interpretation. But regardless of the transcripts' validity, there is reason to believe that Saddam's calculations were not way off the mark. After all, President George H. W. Bush "appeared on television the morning of August 2 [following the invasion of Kuwait] and dismissed military action, declaring that 'we're not discussing intervention.'"[14] For a moment, Saddam seemed to have made the right assumption, that America wouldn't expend the necessary political or military capital to eject him from Kuwait.

As Saddam walked the gallows on December 6, 2006, three and a half years after his government was deposed by the U.S. invasion, he had the last laugh by simply becoming a memory. The 47 percent of the Iraqi population that is under the age of fifteen will hardly remember their country's dictatorial tormentor twenty years from now.[15] But they will remember America, and the scars leftover from a poorly thought-out enterprise that tore Iraq to pieces.

Ideally, America will be able to realign its thinking toward a more prudent outlook: one of basic analyses of power relationships, rather than claims of an "axis of evil," as George W. Bush referred to Iraq, Iran, and North Korea in his 2002 State of the Union address. Only after grasping the basics can we begin to clear the noise of religious language that colors today's Iraqi conflict. But the basics might also humble us. After all, the Iraq War, which touched off the current violence, was a war of choice, based on bombastic ideas about "evil" countries and "good" countries, fundamentalists and moderates, rational versus irrational actors. Had we not forgotten what the thinkers of yesteryear knew, the equations involving a stronger power standing before a weaker one—Group A staring down Group B—we would have never invaded Iraq, and the Sunni-Shia conflict may have never reached its current proportions.

Identities at War

It can be a difficult notion to accept: regardless of our religious or cultural background, any of us have the propensity to take part in civil war, ethnic cleansing, and even genocide; but at the same time, we are equally capable of stopping these horrors. What makes this proposition so problematic is the very thing that makes us fight one another, namely, our connection and devotion to our identity. We are convinced that we are special. *They* kill indiscriminately; *we* fight nobly. But who exactly is they, and who are we?

Identities, our we, can be formed in a variety of ways. Tonight, driving down the I-95 at the wheel of a big rig is Jim. Jim is forty years old and married to a hardworking and always-giddy waitress named Cathy. They have two daughters, Jennifer and Sue. Jim grew up in suburban New Jersey, just outside of Philadelphia, PA. He was a lineman in high school, though his football team was nothing to brag about.

Can you imagine Jim? Jim is working-class through and through. He loves burgers, will kill for a good sports game, especially one involving the New York Jets—a team he's been following religiously since childhood. And speaking of religion, Jim is a Catholic. He doesn't go to church but did have his First Communion, and he and Cathy tied the knot in his hometown parish. Did I mention that Jim is Irish? His family was one of the thousands that followed their dreams to America, making it to Ellis Island in July 1900 with a single suitcase and sorrowful memories of a little girl who had died en route to the New World.

Ever since John F. Kennedy was elected the first Catholic president of the United States in 1960, Jim's family has been staunchly Democratic, and Jim has kept the tradition, voting the party line since he was old enough to do so. And like his father, Jim dreams of retiring with a pension and of trying, hopefully with more success than his father had, to see his kids off to college. That's Jim. That's who he is.

So, is Jim an American, an Irish American, a Christian, a Catholic Christian, a Jets fan, a Caucasian, a father, a married man, a truck driver, a working-class man, a Northeasterner, or a Democrat? Can he not be all those things at the same time? What about a Northeastern banker who works on Wall Street? Is he really that much like Jim? Not until they meet in line at a Los Angeles supermarket, recognize each other's accents, and start complaining about the ways of the West Coast. Then, maybe, for that moment, they are kin.

But on September 11, 2001, the Angelinos in that store would have been kin as well, joining in their sorrow as one nation. Our identities all depend on the situation at hand. They are adaptive, malleable. Nobody would suggest that we can place Jim in a perfect category. So then, what is a Sunni, and what is a Shia? This is no easier to answer than the question of who Jim is.

Immediately following the Cold War, the world, and especially the former communist bloc, seemed to be splitting into pieces. Yugoslavia in particular bore the brunt of this so-called centrifugal phenomenon, with a resurgent nationalism that included calls to separate Bosnia, Slovenia, and Croatia from the rest of the country.

The Balkans wars of the 1990s betrayed a sense that hatred had always existed between the various factions but had been suppressed by the heavy hand of Josef Tito, the erstwhile communist dictator. But identities are anything but constant. Our self-image is like a kaleidoscope, writes Günther Schlee of Germany's Max Planck Institute, that we can turn at any moment to view different aspects of who we are. "There is no end to the kaleidoscopic recombination of features in this game of identity and difference."[16] If Serbian Christians always hated Muslim Bosnians, they weren't necessarily always obsessing over their hatred. At various times during the long Cold War, Bosnian and Serbian families were simply proud Yugoslavians, and little more than that. They could simply turn the kaleidoscope to see their compatriots for who they were.

At the end of the day, what we want to understand is not necessarily how a large inventory of social and national identities can exist within each and every one of us, but how this can translate into people killing each other. For this, we have to return to the issue of Group A versus Group B. It is not that Serbs always wanted to kill Muslim Bosnians but were prevented from doing so by an overpowering dictator. It is rather when state power fails, and a power vacuum ensues, that fear overtakes logic and the impulse for basic group survival kicks in.

Barry Posen of the Massachusetts Institute of Technology has delved into the topic of nonstate violence, applying the "security dilemma" concept to ethnic conflict. A "security dilemma," by traditional definition, is an all-too-common situation in which a state's policy toward greater security ironically leads it to a less secure position. Typically, this occurs when a country builds up its defenses with no intention other than to be secure in its own borders. Yet because most military systems (save for a moat around a castle) can be used for both defensive and offensive operations, the mere fact that a country is building up its military may cause an adversary to build up its own, and perhaps even contemplate a preventive military strike.

In a classic security dilemma, Group A is afraid that Group B is building up its power to strike, so Group A may strike first. The irony lies in the fact that the very thing that Group B was trying to avoid became a reality because of its own actions. Posen writes, "What seems sufficient to one state's defense will seem, and will often be, offensive to its neighbors."[17] It is exactly because the world is anarchic by nature that states cannot afford to "wait and see" on a potential adversary's intentions. In the absence of perfect information, they are inclined to strike first, if only because offensive war is more effective than defensive postures. This fact makes the security dilemma all the more harrowing.

When it comes to ethnic and sectarian conflict, the breakdown of the state creates exactly this kind of anarchic reality. There is no overriding, powerful entity to keep the peace. There are only factions of varying strength and weakness. It is especially the weak who cannot afford to wait and see. They strike. This was true of Serbs in Bosnia and Kosovo, where they are a minority.

In Iraq too, the Sunnis, once dominant but always a minority in the country, had the most to fear from a newly empowered Shia state following the 2003 U.S. invasion. Recruits from around the Sunni world, including al-Qaeda fighters from Saudi Arabia, Libya, and elsewhere in the region, arrived in Iraq to blow themselves up in Shia markets, to decimate Shia places of worship, behead random individuals, and otherwise attempt to disrupt Shia majority rule. Among the most atrocious attacks in the Iraqi civil war was the bombing of the al-Askari Mosque in Samarra, on February 22, 2006. Today, commentators point to this act of Sunni-on-Shia violence as the spark that ignited the Iraqi civil war in earnest. ("That single act of violence would change everything," wrote Fred Barnes of The *Weekly Standard*.[18]) But more than anything, the bombing was "a reflection ... not a cause" of the sectarian violence.[19] The civil war was written in the cards of that country as soon as the invasion began on March 20, 2003, given the delicate power relationships and communal hostilities on the ground.

Let's now briefly return to Jim. Jim, the Catholic, the American, the Caucasian, the Irish—who Jim is, is difficult to say. But what we do know is that when pushed, Jim will likely be willing to fight, and even die, for his people. But who are his people? Are they his fellow Americans, fellow parishioners, his family, or Irish Americans?

Whether countries fight, or whether ethnic groups or religious sects fight, conflict is always based on the given identity held by the group. At any given moment, an individual's identity, as he or she feels it to be in that instance, is worth killing and even dying for. This reality, this break-up of humankind into shattered pieces of self-invented identities, is the story of political conflict itself.

It is in this context that we can begin to understand the Sunni-Shia conflict, one of countless phenomena buried deeply within peaceful communities, ready to emerge at a time of insecurity, provocation, or instigation. One such instigation, the most painful of all, is the kind that takes place when nations are born from the ground up. This is a time, when a land turns into a blank slate and a particular ethnic or religious group believes it can fashion a country after itself, that some of the darkest chapters of human history are written.

The Birth of Nations

"For us," said one of the countless perpetrators of the Rwanda genocide, "kind words for Tutsis were more fatal that evil deeds."[20] Despite having been part of the fabric of the same country, the Tutsis and Hutus of

Rwanda had for centuries been mutually suspicious, even hateful neighbors, bosom enemies living side-by-side. But through bad fate and colonial design, they were pushed into superior/inferior roles that set them up for anything but peaceful coexistence. The Hutus and Tutsis of Rwanda made up a country, but they were never a single nation. They were destined to fight.

But what, after all, is a nation? What is a state, an ethnicity, a tribe, or a family? These are units created by humans to distinguish groups from one another. They can be a motivating factor for cohesion and survival, just as they can create divisiveness and death. Human differences are at once what make us strong and what make us weak, violent, and utterly inhuman.

Regardless of what makes people appear different to one another, it is the breakdown of state power, as it occurred following the collapse of the communist regime in Yugoslavia or the toppling of the Baathist regime in Iraq, that leaves individuals in a particularly vulnerable position and invites violence as a means of self-preservation. Lacking state power, the normal impulse is to seek refuge among one's coreligionists or fellow members of an ethnic group: the Kurds go with the Kurds, the Sunnis with the Sunnis, the Shias with the Shias. Survival dictates separation.

On the eve of the genocide, race acted as a primordial base of identity in Rwanda. Roman Catholics split along Hutu and Tutsi lines, leaving the question of religious unity to a later chapter in history. But in Iraq, where Arabs make up the vast majority of the inhabitants, sectarian lines separated Arab from Arab into the Sunni and Shia camps.

One of the most important characteristics of both ethnic and sectarian conflict is the alienization of others. In Lebanon, Iraq, and Bahrain, Arab Shias are often referred to as "Persians" or "Iranians" by their fellow Arabs as a means of making them into something alien. This is a critical development in a conflict because the more alien a sectarian group is perceived as being, the easier it becomes to dehumanize it and eventually murder its members.

Writing on the Rwanda genocide and its colonial roots, Mahmood Mamdani describes the Hamitic Hypothesis, taken from the Biblical story of Noah's son Ham, as a way of explaining how ethnic groups can come to be classified as "alien." In that story, Ham was cursed for seeing his father drunk and naked. The rabbinical traditions later tell that the House of Ham came to be wretched and "black." The Belgians, like the other European colonialists, embraced a view of Hamite "blacks" who were only superficially so, and thus superior to the "true" Africans—the "Negroes."

The Belgian administration associated the Tutsis in Rwanda with the possession of more "noble" qualities. In their appearance, they were taller and thinner. In their complexion, they were perceived as fairer. Most important, they were a dominant group, and thus the Belgians imagined they had come from some faraway land, perhaps from the House of Ham, to rule and provide whatever iota of civilization had been granted to the Hutus—again, the "real" Africans.

Mamdani traces the pattern of "racialization" in which the differences between Hutu and Tutsi were institutionalized into the colony. But that very differentiation, that alienation of Tutsi as external and superior, later returned to haunt the entire nation. While the Tutsi were placed at the top of the pyramid politically, they "found themselves occupying the bottom rung of a hierarchy of alien races in the colonial period."[21] This is important because, as Mamdani states, the difference between ethnic and racial war is a critical one. The Rwandan genocide, he writes, "needs to be understood as a natives' genocide. It was a genocide by those who saw themselves as sons—and daughters—of the soil, and their mission as one of clearing the soil of a threatening alien presence. This was not an 'ethnic' but a 'racial' cleansing, not a violence against one who is seen as a neighbor but against one who is seen as a foreigner."[22]

To this day, the idea of alien Albanian Muslims has colored Serb claims over the now independent state of Kosovo. The Battle of Kosovo (1389) between Ottomans and Serbs granted the land a mythical status to nationalist Serbs of later years, and it influenced the anti-Kosovar propaganda that led to the massive killings of Muslims in the late 1990s.

The idea of Serbia defending Christian lands from alien Ottomans, however, obscured the fact that not only were fourteenth-century Ottomans often present in Europe at the invitation of various kingdoms, but more important, most of those who later became Muslims were native converts from Christianity, not invading "hordes" from the East. Christian Serbs who did reside in Kosovo, in fact, held "a very vague national consciousness" before 1878,[23] and only later, through the promotion, insistence, and propaganda of Serbian and Russian diplomats, did the concept of Serbian nationhood for Kosovar Christians begin to take root. When Serbian president Slobodan Milosevic oversaw the systematic killing and raping of Kosovar Albanians in 1998, he was in essence trying to undo Serbia's defeat in 1389. He was Christianizing the land, cleansing it of foreign elements.

But how do the perpetrators know whom to target? It turns out that in the midst of cleansing campaigns, figuring out whom to victimize is normally not a problem, and in fact "history records almost no instances of mistaken 'cleansing' of co-ethnics."[24] In the case of religious identity, place of residence can be a good indicator. For example, one who lives in Beirut's Ashrafiye neighborhood is likely a Christian, whereas one who lives in Baghdad's Sadr City is likely a Shia Muslim. Though the former neighborhood is less homogenous than the latter, a confessional assumption can nevertheless be made.

In the case of mixed neighborhoods, names provide clues as to a person's sectarian tendencies. The names "Ali" and "Fatima," for example, are considered typical Shia names, whereas Umar, Aisha, and Yazid are quintessentially Sunni. When all else fails, simple intelligence, acquired over the years—the observance of certain holidays, the company a neighbor keeps, etc.—helps potential aggressors know their victims before they strike. In postwar Iraq, Muqtada al-Sadr's operatives have been known to draw up lists of "virtuous" Shias in certain neighborhoods, as well as Sunnis targeted for expulsion or death.[25] In extreme cases, those who foresee a fight will actually draw up "hit lists" years in advance. (In 2008, a former Christian militia officer admitted to me in the mountains of Lebanon that he had drawn up such a list of his neighbors, to be used once the next civil war breaks out.)

Ethnic and sectarian conflict is inherently tied to a pursuit of domination, and in extreme cases, even state creation. To alienate a people from a land is to help make that land into a homeland for oneself. There have been thousands upon thousands of "peoples" in the world, but only a few have achieved their own viable states. In the Middle East these states have been taken over by extended families, while in Europe ethnic groups have come to dominate. Killing, pillaging, and raping to create a country has been as common to history as war itself, and it would be foolish to think that this practice is simply going to fade into obscurity.

A visceral illustration of the birth pangs of state creation is the founding of the ancient Land of Israel, as recounted in the Bible. Such a bloody endeavor had to be seen as divinely sanctioned if it were ever to be legitimized in memory. The Book of Numbers recounts the story of the conquest of Canaan, when God harkened "to the voice of Israel, and delivered up the Canaanites; and they utterly destroyed them and their cities" (21:3). Prior to crossing the Jordan, the People of Israel left their mark on the unforgiving political landscape of antiquity. During their war with the Midians, they did away with every male, though this hardly satisfied Moses. He ordered his troops to "kill every male among the little ones, and kill every woman that hath known man by lying with him" (31:17). Virgin women were left for the soldiers to keep. This was the story of Israel's Biblical birth, but it could have been that of any other nation. Even in Europe, "most of the history of state formation," as Lisa Anderson reminds us, "is a history of cruelty and coercion."[26]

Ethnic, religious, and racial strife can be viewed from various angles. It can be seen as a series of irrational acts of hatred, or as paranoid pushes toward self-preservation. It can, in some cases, be seen as an attempt to form a nation from scratch within a particular territory, and thus it can hold some trace of rationality, however tragic and stomach-turning. On the process of successful state creation in Europe, Charles Tilly wrote:

> Almost all European governments eventually took steps which homogenized their populations: the adoption of state religions, expulsion of minorities like the Moors and the Jews, institu-

tion of a national language, eventually the organization of mass public instruction. ... The failure to homogenize increased the likelihood that a state existing at a given point in time would fragment into its cultural subdivisions at some time in the future.[27]

Obviously, such a statement could be misconstrued to mean that states should not be multicultural, but that is not the point. The idea is that when states are forming, they desperately need a glue that will hold them together through the rough times. This glue can be a unifying ethno-linguistic theme, a religion, or, as it was in the case of the United States, a common political culture. In Iraq, as in Lebanon, there is hardly enough glue to keep the house in order. Both countries were arbitrarily created by European powers, and both were built on territories that mixed ethnic and religious groups that shared a common hatred and little else.

Genocide, the most unspeakable crime known to man, is normally associated with these very forces of state-formation. The Holocaust is rarely spoken of in these terms, but it is one example of such impulses to "cleanse" a land that is reinventing itself on a massive scale. Germany, as a politically unified state did not truly come about until 1871, on the heels of the Franco-Prussian War. And it wasn't until World War II that it sought to unify all ethnic Germans, including those of Austria and regions of Poland and Czechoslovakia, under one roof. Like state formation in centuries past, such as the forced Christianization of Spain during the *Reconquista* and the Inquisition, the virtual wiping out of Native Americans in what is now the United States, and the genocide of Armenians during the birth of modern Turkey, Germany as a nation for *all* Germans was only coming to being in the 1930s, employing sectarian hatred on the most horrific of terms.

Jewish communities across Europe, which held a cultural affinity to Germany, via their speech, food, and family names, were nevertheless targets of a sectarian cleansing campaign that mechanized and industrialized genocide on a level never witnessed before.

There may never be another Holocaust, but the kind of forces that brought it about have not been extinguished. The real question pending for the world is whether Lebanon and Iraq, two arbitrary states sharing a painful legacy of sectarian divisions, may be in the process of building new, real nations from scratch. If so, the pain and destruction seen thus far could very well be a prelude for more horrific things to come. The United States should cast aside any hope for an ideal outcome of democracy in the Land between the Rivers, and instead plan and work tirelessly to avoid the human catastrophe that is state-formation in its most organic form. That is the least that America, which reshuffled the ethnic and sectarian deck of cards of an entire country, can, and should do.

Notes

Prologue: What Is Islam?

1. W. Montgomery Watt, *Muhammad: Prophet and Statesman* (London: Oxford University Press, 1974), 228.

2. Daniel Howden, "The Destruction of Mecca: Saudi Hardliners Are Wiping Out Their Own Heritage," *The Independent*, August 6, 2005.

Chapter 1: The Three Catalysts

1. The author witnessed the scene on Martyr's Square in July 2008. The quote by Robert Fisk is from *Pity the Nation: The Abduction of Lebanon* (New York: Nation Books, 2002), 77.

2. Fisk, *Pity the Nation*, 76.

3. "Mubarak's Shia Remarks Stir Anger," *Iraqi News*, April 10, 2006.

4. "Saudi Clerics Criticize Shiites for Destabilizing," *Associated Press*, June 1, 2008.

5. Qaradawi quoted in Jeffrey Fleishman, "Egyptian Sheik's Outburst against Shiites Roils Mideast," *Los Angeles Times*, September 28,

2008.

6. See "Poll: Nasrallah Most Admired Leader in Arab World," *Jerusalem Post*, July 16, 2008.

Chapter 2: The Battleground

1. Susan Wise Bauer, *History of the Ancient World: From the Earliest Accounts to the Fall of Rome* (New York: Norton, 2007), 18. The name "Iraq," writes Bernard Lewis, "in medieval Arab usage was that of a province, consisting of the southern half of the present country of that name from Takrit southwards toward the sea. It was sometimes also called 'Iraq 'Arabi to distinguish it from 'Iraq 'Ajami, the adjoining area of southwestern Iran." Bernard Lewis, *The Middle East: 2,000 Years of History from the Rise of Christianity to the Present Day* (London: Weidenfeld & Nicholson, 1995), 22–23.

2. George Roux, *Ancient Iraq* (Harmondsworth, UK: Penguin, 1964), 56–57.

3. Ibid., 22.

4. Jared Diamond, *Guns, Germs, and Steel: The Fates of Human Societies* (New York: Norton, 1997), ch. 10.

5. Colin S. Gray, *The Geopolitics of Super Power* (Lexington: University Press of Kentucky, 1988), 15.

6. C. V. Wedgwood, *The Thirty Years War* (London: Penguin Books, 1957), 33–34.

7. Mark Whittow, *The Making of Orthodox Byzantium, 600–1025* (Berkeley: University of California Press, 1996), 30.

8. Jonathan Berkey, *The Formation of Islam: Religion and Society in the Near East, 600–1800* (Cambridge, UK: Cambridge University Press, 2002), 47–48. On Ctesiphon as the capital of the Sassanid Empire, see Jens Kröger, "Ctesiphon," *Encyclopaedia Iranica Online*, 1993, http://www.iranica.com.

9. Stephen Williams and Gerard Friell, *The Rome That Did Not Fall: The Survival of the East in the Fifth Century* (London: Routledge,

1999), 55.

10. Warren Treadgold, A Concise History of Byzantium (Houndmills, Basingstoke, Hampshire: Palgrave, 2001), 89.

Chapter 3: The Message and the Messengers

1. Reza Aslan, *No God but God: The Origins, Evolution, and Future of Islam* (New York: Random House, 2005), 106

2. Alison Frantz, "From Paganism to Christianity in the Temples of Athens," Dumbarton Oaks Papers 19 (1965): 186. On the death penalty, see Michele Renee Salzman, "The Evidence for the Conversion of the Roman Empire to Christianity in Book 16 of the 'Theodosian Code,'" *Historia: Zeitschrift für Alte Geschichte* 42, no. 3 (1993): 369.

3. Berkey, *Formation of Islam*, 21.

4. For an unbiased and thorough account of the early Muslim conquests, see Hugh Kennedy, *The Great Arab Conquests: How the Spread of Islam Changed the World We Live In* (New York: Da Capo Press, 2007)

5. Moojan Momen quoting Ibn Hanbal from a Sunni collection of Hadiths. This episode is used by Shias to illustrate the designation of Ali as successor to the Prophet. See Moojan Momen, *An Introduction to Shi'i Islam: The History and Doctrines of Twelver Shi'ism* (New Haven: Yale University Press, 1985), 15.

6. Patricia Crone, *God's Rule—Government and Islam: Six Centuries of Medieval Islamic Political Thought* (New York: Columbia University Press, 2005), 18.

7. See G. R. Hawting, *The First Dynasty of Islam: The Umayyad Caliphate AD 661–750*, 2nd ed. (London: Routledge, 2000), ch. 2. Also see Martin Hinds, "The Murder of the Caliph 'Uthman," *International Journal of Middle East Studies* 3, no. 4 (October 1972), 450–69.

8. Some insights can be found in Hamid Dabashi, *Authority in Islam: From the Rise of Muhammad to the Establishment of the Umayyads* (New Brunswick, NJ: Transaction Publishers, 1989)

9. S. H. M. Jafri, quoted in Momen, *Introduction to Shi'i Islam*, 32.

Chapter 4: The Fault Lines

1. Andrew J. Newman, *Formative Period of Twelver Shi'ism: Hadith as Discourse between Qum and Baghdad* (Richmond, Surrey: Curzon, 2000), 2.

2. Ira M. Lapidus, "The Separation of State and Religion in the Development of Early Islamic Society," *International Journal of Middle East Studies* 6, no. 4 (1975): 372.

3. Hugh Kennedy, *Early Abbasid Caliphate: A Political History* (London: Croom Helm, 1981), p. 157. Also see Patricia Crone, *God's Rule—Government and Islam: Six Centuries of Medieval Islamic Political Thought* (New York: Columbia University Press, 2005), 93. On Ma'mun's fondness of the Imam, see Wilferd Madelung, "'Ali al-Reza," *Encyclopaedia Iranica Online*, 1985, http://www.iranica.com.

4. Hugh Kennedy, writing about the early Abbasids, explains, "The propaganda which recruited supporters for the revolutionary army was very broadly based, appealing simply for a *rida* (chosen one) from the family of the Prophet. There was no need to spell out a detailed programme of reform; if the family of Muhammad ruled, and the Qur'an was obeyed, all other problems which beset the community and gave rise to so much discontent would naturally solve themselves." Kennedy, *Early Abbasid Caliphate*, 158.

5. Ibid., p. 42.

6. Crone, *God's Rule*, 89.

7. Kennedy, *Early Abbasid Caliphate*, 43.

8. Crone, *God's Rule*, 94.

9. The word *bagh* in Baghdad does not refer to a "garden," as modern Persian would imply, but to the Old Iranian *baga*, meaning "god." See Hugh Kennedy, "Baghdad," *Encyclopaedia Iranica Online*, 1989, http://www.iranica.com. For more on the *barid*, see Kennedy, Early

Abbasid Caliphate, 157.

10. Gaston Wiet, *Baghdad: Metropolis of the Abbasid Caliphate*, trans. Seymour Feiler (Norman: University of Oklahoma Press, 1971), 16–17.

11. Quoted in Ibid., 21.

12. J. T. P. de Bruijn, "Courts and Courtiers," *Encyclopaedia Iranica Online*, 1993, http://www.iranica.com. Even Caliph Ma'mun was known for having Persian royal texts translated. He then used the texts to learn about governance and the ways of the Iranian court. See Michael Cooperson, *Al-Ma'mun* (Oxford: One World, 2005), 32–33.

13. See George Makdisi, "The Significance of Sunni Schools of Law in Islamic Religious History," *International Journal of Middle East Studies* 10, no. 1 (1979); On the Sunni debate over ijtihad, see Wael B. Hallaq, "Was the Gate of Ijtihad Closed?" *International Journal of Middle East Studies* 16, no. 1 (1984). The mere fact that such an article had to be written betrays a general consensus that the Sunni practice of ijtihad is limited.

14. Seyyed Vali Reza Nasr, *The Shia Revival: How Conflicts within Islam Will Shape the Future* (New York: Norton, 2006), 73.

15. Quoted in Alice Hunsberger, *Nasir Khusraw, the Ruby of Badakhshan: A Portrait of the Persian Poet, Traveller, and Philosopher* (London: I. B. Tauris, 2003), 58.

16. Quoted in Heinz Halm, Shi'ism, 2nd ed. (New York: Columbia University Press, 2004), 65. Nakash has Ashoura proceedings occurring as early as the ninth century within "public mosques." See Yitzhak Nakash, "An Attempt to Trace the Origin of the Rituals of Ashura," *Die Welt des Islams* 33, no. 2 (1993): 63.

17. Hossein Modarressi, "Rationalism and Traditionalism in Shi'i Jurisprudence: A Preliminary Survey," *Studia Islamica*, no. 59 (1984): 142.

18. Quoted in Halm, *Shi'ism*, 46.

Chapter 5: A Region Divided

1. Bernard Lewis, *The Assassins: A Radical Sect in Islam* (New York: Basic Books, 1968), 31. For more on the weekly lectures, see Paul E. Walker, *Exploring an Islamic Empire: Fatimid History and Its Sources* (London: I. B. Tauris, 2002), 43.

2. Paul E. Walker, "The Ismaili da'wa in the Reign of the Fatimid Caliph al-Hakim," in *Fatimid History and Ismaili Doctrine* (Aldershot, Hampshire: Ashgate/Variorum, 2008), III, 8.

3. In fact, the Iranian people are believed to have entered the Iranian plateau via Khorasan at around 1000 BC. Khorasan is not a defined place, but a general region with boundaries that have shifted throughout history and that have been subjectively defined by writers of different eras. See Christine Noelles-Karimi, "Khurasan and Its Limits: Changing Concepts of Territory from Pre-Modern to Modern Times," in *Iran und iranisch geprägte Kulturen*, ed. Markus Ritter, Ralph Kauz, and Birgitt Hoffmann (Wiesbaden: Reichert, 2008). On the Iranian people's migration into the plateau, see Clement Huart, *Ancient Persia and Iranian Civilization* (New York: Knopf, 1927), 26. Regarding the Seljuk entrance into the region, see chapter 3 in David Morgan, *Medieval Persia 1040–1797* (London: Longman, 1988). Note that Seljuks first ruled Byzantine lands as a Muslim minority, ruling over a Christian faithful. See Elizavet A. Zachariadou, "Religious Dialogue Between Byzantines and the Turks during the Ottoman Expansion," in *Studies in Pre-Ottoman Turkey and the Ottomans* (Aldershot, Hampshire: Ashgate/Variorum, 2004).

4. Heinz Halm, *Shi'ism*, 2nd ed. (New York: Columbia University Press, 2004), 58–59.

5. See Moojan Momen, *An Introduction to Shi'i Islam: The History and Doctrines of Twelver Shi'ism* (New Haven: Yale University Press, 1985), 90.

6. This is a simplification. For details on Seljuk spread of the Sunni madrasa, see Wilferd Madelung, "The Spread of Maturidism and the Turks," in *Actas, IV Congresso de Estudos Arabes e Islámicos*, Coimbra-Lisboa 1 a 8 de septembro de 1968 (Leiden: E. J. Brill, 1971). When

Salah al-Din came to power, he began the process of embracing various branches of Sunnism concurrently. This process was later continued by the Mamluk dynasties. See Yehoshu'a Frenkel, "Political and Social Aspects of Islamic Religious Endowments ("awqaf"): Saladin in Cairo (1169–73) and Jerusalem (1187–93)," *Bulletin of the School of Oriental and African Studies* 62, no. 1 (1999)

7. Reuven Amitai-Preiss, *Mongols and Mamluks: The Mamluk-Ilkhanid War, 1260–1281* (Cambridge: Cambridge University Press, 1995), 10.

8. Madelung, "Spread of Maturidism and the Turks," 164. Note that Salah al-Din is not a Seljuk per se, but the founder of the short-lived Ayyubid dynasty.

9. Amitai-Preiss, *Mongols and Mamluks*, 36.

10. David C. Rapoport, "Fear and Trembling: Terrorism in Three Religious Traditions," *American Political Science Review* 78, no. 3 (1984): 666.

11. Albert Hourani gives credit to Jabal Amil's remoteness and difficulty to conquer for some of the productive development in Shia learning that occurred there. See Hourani, "From Jabal Amil to Persia," *Bulletin of the School of Oriental and African Studies* 49, no. 1 (1986): 134.

12. Quoted in Tomaz Mastnak, "Europe and the Muslims: The Permanent Crusade?" in *The New Crusades: Constructing the Muslim Enemy*, ed. Emran Qureshi and Michael A. Sells (New York: Columbia University Press, 2003), 210–11.

13. Ibid., 207.

14. H. R. Roemer, "The Safavid Period," in ed. Peter Jackson, *The Cambridge History of Iran*, Vol. 6 (Cambridge: Cambridge University Press, 1986), 193.

15. Said Amir Arjomand, *The Shadow of God and the Hidden Imam: Religion, Political Order, and Societal Change in Shi'ite Iran from the Beginning to 1890* (Chicago: University of Chicago Press, 1984), 162.

16. Andrew J. Newman, *Safavid Iran: Rebirth of a Persian Empire* (London: I. B. Tauris, 2006), 38. On the observation of Nowrooz at the Safavid court, see Goto Yukako, "The Safavid Court and Its Cermonies during the Reign of Muhammad Khudabande," in *Iran und iranisch geprägte Kulturen*.

17. Rosemary Stanfield Johnson, "Sunni Survival in Safavid Iran: Anti-Sunni Activities during the Reign of Tahmasp I," *Iranian Studies* 27, no. 1 (1994): 125. For more on the inclusion of Ali in the call to prayer, see Liyakat A. Takim, "From Bid'a to Sunna: The Wilaya of 'Ali in the Shi'i Adhan," *Journal of the American Oriental Society* 120, no. 2 (2000), especially p. 170.

18. Madeline C. Zilfi, "The Ottoman ulema," in ed. Suraiya N. Faroqhi, *The Cambridge History of Turkey*, Vol. 3 (Cambridge: Cambridge University Press, 2006), 210.

19. Carl Max Kortepeter, *Ottoman Imperialism during the Reformation: Europe and the Caucasus* (New York: New York University Press, 1972). See ch. 3.

20. Yitzhak Nakash, *The Shi'is of Iraq*, 2nd ed. (Princeton, NJ: Princeton University Press, 2003), 254. See also pp. 25–28.

21. Vanessa Martin, "Religion and State in Khumaini's 'Kashf al-asrar,'" *Bulletin of the School of Oriental and African Studies* 56, no. 1 (1993): 35. Martin explains that part of Khomeini's anger stemmed from Wahhabi-related movements at the time, which preached for the individual application of ijtihad (as opposed to the purely clerical kind, as espoused by Shiism).

Chapter 6: An Imagined Land

1. Naomi Klein, *The Shock Doctrine: The Rise of Disaster Capitalism* (New York: Henry Holt, 2007), 322.

2. Twelve people died from the coordinated sarin nerve gas attacks on three rush-hour subways in Tokyo. In contrast, the Madrid commuter train attacks of March 11, 2004, which made use of conven-

tional explosives, killed 191. The reason for this disparity in casualties is a matter of physics: one cannot run away from an explosion.

3. On background, from a group discussion with a weapons inspector.

4. Patricia Crone, *Slaves on Horses: The Evolution of the Islamic Polity* (Cambridge: Cambridge University Press, 1980), 23.

5. Peter Sluglett and Marion Farouk-Sluglett, "Some Reflections on the Sunni/Shi'i Question in Iraq," *Bulletin* (British Society for Middle East Studies) 5, no. 2 (1978): 82.

6. Quoted in Peter Sluglett, *Britain in Iraq: Contriving King and Country, 1914–1932* (London: I. B. Tauris, 2007), 23.

7. Quoted in Ibid., 46.

8. Nasr, *The Shia Revival: How Conflicts within Islam Will Shape the Future* (New York: Norton, 2006), 108.

9. Marion Farouk-Sluglett and Peter Sluglett, *Iraq Since 1958: From Revolution to Dictatorship*, rev. ed. (London: I. B. Tauris, 2001), 91–92.

10. Shiva Balaghi, *Saddam Hussein: A Biography* (Westport, CT: Greenwood Press, 2006), 72. The 10 percent figure for the Baath comes from Tarik Kafala, "The Iraqi Baath Party," *BBC News Online*, March 25, 2003, http://news.bbc.co.uk/1/hi/world/middle_east/2886733.stm.

11. From al-Fatawa al-wadiha (Beirut, 1978), as paraphrased in Modarressi, "Rationalism and Traditionalism in Shi'i Jurisprudence," 142.

12. The document was *Manabi' al-Qudra fi-d Dawla al-Islamiyya* (Sources of Power in the Islamic State). See Chibli Mallat, *The Renewal of Islamic Law: Muhammad Baqer as-Sadr, Najaf, and the Shi'i International* (Cambridge: Cambridge University Press, 1993), 69–73.

13. See for example Hamid Dabashi, *Theology of Discontent: The Ideological Foundation of the Islamic Republic of Iran* (New Brunswick, NJ: Transaction Publishers, 2006), 413.

14. Iran's political system is not, as many commentators suggest,

a dictatorship. It can best be imagined as a secretive but fluid and relatively weak oligarchy sitting atop a democratic-republican system. The religious oligarchy allows the republic to function, but it limits the latter's ability to institute reforms and maintain independence by rigging the judiciary, constraining the powers of the elected president, and vetting candidates before they can run for office. Once candidates are vetted, however, they engage in vigorous electoral contestation in a process that reflects Iran's long-running trend of civic participation and grassroots political engagement.

15. Patrick Cockburn, *Muqtada: Muqtada al-Sadr, the Shia Revival, and the Struggle for Iraq* (New York: Scribner, 2008), 52. On the deaths of Baqir and Bint al-Huda, see p. 28.

16. Hussein Sirriyeh, *U.S. Policy in the Gulf, 1968–1977: Aftermath of British Withdrawal* (London: Ithaca Press, 1984), 62.

17. Ofra Bengio, *Saddam's Word: Political Discourse in Iraq* (New York: Oxford University Press, 1998), 81.

18. Shahram Chubin and Charles Tripp, *Iran and Iraq at War* (Boulder, CO: Westview Press, 1988), 23.

19. Cockburn, *Muqtada*, 49.

20. Ibid., 63.

21. Quoted in Ibid., 66.

22. The video of the C-SPAN interview is widely available on YouTube, and was first posted by grandtheftcountry. The transcript used here is from the website *A Tiny Revolution*, http://www.tinyrevolution.com/mt/archives/001662.html.

23. Jalil Roshandel, "Iran's Foreign and Security Policies: How the Decision-making Process Evolved," *Security Dialog*, 31, no. 1 (March 2000)

24. Figures of Iraqi expenditures actually come from a study of Iran's military by Anthony Cordesman, in which the author juxtaposes military spending between the two North Gulf countries. See Cordesman, "Iran's Evolving Military Forces," Center for Strategic and International Studies, July 2004, 6. Figures for Iran and Saudi Arabia in

2002 appear as percentages of GDP in the 2002 *CIA World Factbook* (Saudi figures are taken from fiscal year 2000).

25. Mohammad Khatami, interview with Christiane Amanpour, CNN, January 7, 1998.

26. "Letter to President Clinton on Iraq," Project for the New American Century, January 26, 1998, http://www.newamericancentury.org/iraqclintonletter.htm.

27. *NewsHour with Jim Lehrer*, PBS, February 11, 1998.

28. See, for example, "On Tape, Hussein Talks of WMDs," CNN.com, February 19, 2006, http://www.cnn.com/2006/WORLD/meast/02/18/hussein.tapes/index.html.

Chapter 7: The First Iraq

1. Sandra Mackey, *Lebanon: A House Divided* (New York: Norton, 2006), 24.

2. David C. Gordon, *Lebanon: The Fragmented Nation* (London: Croom Helm, 1980), 148. Robert Fisk writes of how Pierre Gemayel, eventual leader of the Phalange Christian militia, formed a youth movement fashioned after Nazi Germany's Hitler Jugend following a visit to Berlin during the 1936 Olympics: "And I saw then discipline and order. And I said to myself: 'Why can't we do the same thing in Lebanon?' So when we came back to Lebanon, we created this youth movement." Fisk, *Pity the Nation: The Abduction of Lebanon* (New York: Nation Books, 2002), 64.

3. See Nathan Gonzalez, *Engaging Iran: The Rise of a Middle East Powerhouse and America's Strategic Choice* (Westport, CT: Praeger, 2007), 102.

4. Fisk, *Pity the Nation*, 63.

5. Kais M. Firro, *Inventing Lebanon: Nationalism and the State under the Mandate* (London: I. B. Tauris, 2003), 120.

6. Thomas L. Friedman, *From Beirut to Jerusalem* (New York: Anchor Books, 1995), 13.

7. Mackey, *Lebanon*, 163.

8. Fisk, *Pity the Nation*, 79.

9. Ibid., 76.

10. "Sabra and Shatila 20 Years On," *BBC News*, September 14, 2002, http://news.bbc.co.uk/2/hi/middle_east/2255902.stm

11. Fisk, 360–61.

Chapter 8: Chaos and Promise

1. Anthony H. Cordesman, *The Iraq War: Strategy, Tactics, and Military Lessons* (Westport, CT: Praeger, 2003), ch. 4.

2. Fiachra Gibbons, "Experts Mourn the Lion of Nimrud, Looted as Troops Stood By," *Guardian*, April 30, 2003.

3. Thomas E. Ricks, *Fiasco: The American Military Adventure in Iraq* (New York: Penguin Books, 2007), 111.

4. Peter W. Galbraith, *The End of Iraq: How American Incompetence Created a War Without End* (New York: Simon & Schuster, 2006), 119.

5. Ali A. Allawi, *The Occupation of Iraq: Winning the War, Losing the Peace* (New Haven, CT: Yale University Press, 2007), 150.

6. Brian Fishman, ed., *Bombers, Bank Accounts & Bleedout: al-Qa'ida's Road In and Out of Iraq*, Harmony Project, Combating Terrorism Center at West Point, 2008.

7. "Foreign Fighters in Iraq Are Tied to U.S. Allies," The *New York Times* (November 22, 2007)

8. "Egypt Removes Iraq Pro-insurgency Channel from Air," *Reuters*, February 26, 2007.

9. "Najaf bombing kills Shiite leader, followers say," CNN, August 30, 2003.

10. Thomas E. Ricks, *The Gamble: General David Petraeus and the American Military Adventure in Iraq, 2006-2008* (New York: Penguin Press, 2009), 322

11. Patrick Cockburn, *Muqtada: Muqtada al-Sadr, the Shia Re-*

vival, and the Struggle for Iraq (New York: Scribner, 2008), 186.

12. Scott Peterson, "Could Iran Help Stabilize Iraq?" *Christian Science Monitor*, November 15, 2006. The text of the letter can be read in the appendix section of Trita Parsi's *Treacherous Alliance: The Secret Dealings of Israel, Iran, and the United States* (New Haven, CT: Yale University Press, 2008).

13. Allawi, *Occupation of Iraq*, 148.

14. Jack Snyder, *From Voting to Violence: Democratization and Nationalist Conflict* (New York: Norton, 2000), 16.

15. Ibid., 40.

16. Ibid.

17. Samuel P. Huntington, *Political Order in Changing Societies* (New Haven: Yale University Press, 2006), 7.

18. "Guide to Iraqi political parties," *BBC News*, January 20, 2006

19. Independent Commission on the Security Forces of Iraq, *The Report of the Independent Commission on the Security Forces of Iraq* (Washington, DC: Center for Strategic and International Studies, September 6, 2007), 29 (hereafter referred to as the Jones Report).

20. Joseph Felter and Brian Fishman, *Iranian Strategy in Iraq: Politics and 'Other Means'* (West Point, NY: Combating Terrorism Center, U.S. Military Academy at West Point, October 13, 2008), 21.

21. *Iraq's Shi'ites Under Occupation* (Brussels: International Crisis Group, September 9, 2003), quoted in Cockburn, *Muqtada*, 132.

22. Quoted in Cockburn, *Muqtada*, 132.

23. Ibid., 119.

24. Craig Smith, "Aftereffects: Iran's Influence; Cleric in Iran Says Shiites Must Act," *New York Times*, April 26, 2003.

25. Bruce R. Pirnie and Edward O'Connell, *Counterinsurgency in Iraq (2003–2006)* (Santa Monica: RAND National Defense Research Institute, 2008), 32.

26. Anthony H. Cordesman, *Iraq's Sectarian and Ethnic Violence and Its Evolving Insurgency* (Washington, DC: Center for Strategic

and International Studies, April 2, 2007), 104.

27. Pirnie and O'Connell, *Counterinsurgency in Iraq*, 26.

28. Jones Report, 26.

29. The 10 percent figure comes from Pirnie and O'Connell, *Counterinsurgency in Iraq*. This report also claims that despite that estimate, nearly one in four of all prisoners at the Abu Ghraib complex were foreigners in 2005. See p. 29.

30. Brookings Institution, "Iraq Index: Tracking Variables of Reconstruction & Security in Post-Saddam Iraq," February 26, 2009. Calculated using the top four rows of the table: on p. 9 ("Detailed Breakdown of Deaths ...").

31. The 80 percent figure comes from the Jones Report, 28. The Combating Terrorism Center, at the U.S. Military Academy at West Point, analyzed a sample of 595 al-Qaeda-generated personnel records. Of this sample of al-Qaeda in Mesopotamia recruits, 41 percent were of Saudi origin, with the second-highest affiliation being Libyan (18 percent). See Joseph Felter and Brian Fishman, *Al-Qa'ida's Foreign Fighters in Iraq: A First Look at the Sinjar Records* (West Point, NY: Combating Terrorism Center, U.S. Military Academy at West Point, December 19, 2007).

32. Pirnie and O'Connell, *Counterinsurgency in Iraq*, 30.

33. Felter and Fishman, *Iranian Strategy*, 6.

34. Jones Report, 31.

35. Cordesman, *Iraq's Sectarian and Ethnic Violence*, 4. The import figure is from Hassan Baqi, president of the Suleymaniyah Chamber of Commerce. Quoted by "Tensions Mount Between Iraqi Kurdistan, Iran," *All Things Considered*, NPR, September 28, 2007.

36. Quoted in Michael Duffy, "What Would War Look Like?" *Time*, September 17, 2006.

37. See "Cult, Police Clash at Iraqi Religious Rites," Los Angeles Times, January 19, 2008.

38. See Kathleen Ridolfo, "Iraq: Does Government Crackdown Target Messianic Cults or Opposition?" *Globalsecurity.org*, 2008,

http://www.globalsecurity.org/wmd/library/news/iraq/2008/02/
iraq-080206-rferl01.htm.

39. Michael R. Gordon, "Troop 'Surge' Took Place Amid Doubt and
Debate," *New York Times*, August 30, 2008.

40. Ibid.

41. "A Dark Side to Iraq 'Awakening' Groups," *International Herald Tribune*, January 4, 2008.

42. Dexter Filkins, "US Hands Back a Quieter Anbar," *New York Times*, September 1, 2008.

43. Alex Horton, "Enemies with Benefits," *Army of Dude*, July 27,
2008,   http://armyofdude.blogspot.com/2008/07/enemies-with-benefits.html.

44. Richard A. Oppel Jr., "Iraq Takes Aim at U.S.-Tied Sunni
Groups' Leaders," *New York Times*, August 21, 2008.

45."Iraq Militia Chief Condemned to Death for Karbala Killings,"
AFP, August 30, 2008.

46. It is important not to overstate the importance of official titles,
however. The Iranian Revolution of 1978–79 turned religious doctrine
into a politically charged Islamic papacy. While Ayatollah Khomeini
was a highly qualified Islamic theologian in his own right, his successor, Ali Khamene'i, was little more than a political operative, a true believer of the revolution. Khamene'i was a hujjatu al-Islam himself, and
not an ayatollah, before being conspicuously upgraded in 1989 following a hastily assembled meeting in Qom. That same year the Iranian
constitution was amended to allow someone without the title of marja
to become the supreme leader of the revolution, the highest post on the
land.

Higher ranking figures such as Grand Ayatollah Ali Montazeri,
once Khomeini's right hand but relegated to house arrest after splitting politically with the supreme leader, were all but sidelined with the
political ascension of Khamene'i. For years, Montazeri's title of Grand
Ayatollah was stripped in the official media of the Islamic Republic.
Politics consistently trumps theology.

47."Aide: Iraq's al-Sadr May Stay in Iran for Years," *Associated Press*, August 23, 2008.

48. "Loyalists of Iraq's Sadr Sign Blood Oaths to Continue Fighting," *AFP*, August 29, 2008.

Chapter 9: Future of a Region

1. Joseph Felter and Brian Fishman, *Al-Qa'ida's Foreign Fighters in Iraq: A First Look at the Sinjar Records* (West Point, NY: Combating Terrorism Center, U.S. Military Academy at West Point, December 19, 2007).

2. Joseph Felter and Brian Fishman, "Becoming a Foreign Fighter: A Second Look at the Sinjar Records," in Brian Fishman, ed., *Bombers, Bank Accounts & Bleedout: al-Qa'ida's Road In and Out of Iraq*, Harmony Project, Combating Terrorism Center at West Point, 2008.

3. Ron Nordland, "Now It's a Census that Could Rip Iraq Apart," The New York Times (July 25, 2009); The 70-80% figure for the south comes from: "Iraq: Oil," Energy Information Administration, U.S. Department of Energy: http://www.eia.doe.gov/cabs/Iraq/Oil.html

4. Aram Roston, *The Man Who Pushed America to War: The Extraordinary Life, Adventures, and Obsessions of Ahmed Chalabi* (New York: Nation Books, 2008), 314.

Companion Essay: On Human Conflict

1. Ibn Khaldun, *The Muqaddimah: An Introduction to History*. Translated from the Arabic by Franz Rosenthal, edited and abridged by N. J. Dawood (Princeton, NJ: Bollinger / Princeton University Press, 1989), 336

2. For example, Arnaud de Borchgrave, editor-at-large of the *Washington Times* and *United Press International*, wrote in an op-ed, "The mullahs' aim, therefore, with no ifs or buts, is . . . 'the destruction of Israel.'" "Holocaust II?" *Washington Times*, August 11, 2008.

3. Robert A. Pape, "The Strategic Logic of Suicide Terrorism," *American Political Science Review* 97, no. 3 (2003). The book is *Dying to Win: The Strategic Logic of Suicide Terrorism* (New York: Random House, 2005).

4. Paul Kennedy, *The Rise and Fall of the Great Powers: Economic Change and Military Conflict from 1500 to 2000* (New York: Vintage Books, 1989), 515.

5. White House, "President Bush Outlines Iraqi Threat: Remarks by the President on Iraq," news release, October 7, 2002, http://www.whitehouse.gov/news/releases/2002/10/20021007-8.html.

6. "Saddam's Ultimate Solution," Wide Angle, *PBS*, July 11, 2002, http://www.pbs.org/wnet/wideangle/printable/transcript_saddam.html

7. Kenneth M. Pollack, *The Threatening Storm: The Case for Invading Iraq* (New York: Random House, 2002), 250.

8. Ibid., 253.

9. Julian Borger, "Saddam, Tell Me about Your Mum," *Guardian*, November 14, 2002.

10. Pollack, *Threatening Storm*, 253.

11. Rice, quoted in "Rice Says Saddam Evil and Must Be Dealt With," *Japan Today*, August 16, 2002.

12. George A. Lopez and David Cortright, "Containing Iraq: Sanctions Worked," *Foreign Affairs*, July–August 2004. The United States supported Iraq during the Iran-Iraq War, and between 1981 and 1985 it is estimated that Iraq imported up to $24 billion in weaponry from the United States. See "Iraqi Army," *GlobalSecurity.org*, June 22, 2005,

http://www.globalsecurity.org/military/world/iraq/army.htm.

13. "Excerpts from Iraqi Document on Meeting with U.S. Envoy," *New York Times*, September 23, 1990.

14. Daniel S. Papp, "The Gulf War Coalition: The Politics and Economics of a Most Unusual Alliance," in *The Eagle in the Desert: Looking Back on U.S. Involvement in the Persian Gulf War*, ed. William Head and Earl H. Tilford Jr. (Westport, CT: Praeger, 1996), 27.

15. "Iraqi Population Outlook Uncertain," Population Reference Bureau, April 2003, http://www.prb.org/Articles/2003/IraqiPopulationOutlookUncertain.aspx.

16. Günther Schlee, ed., *Imagined Differences: Hatred and the Construction of Identity* (Münster, Germany: Lit Verlag, 2002), 8.

17. Barry R. Posen, "The Security Dilemma and Ethnic Conflict," *Survival* 35, no. 1 (Spring 1993): 28.

18. Fred Barnes, "How Bush Decided on the Surge," *Weekly Standard*, February 4, 2008.

19. Ahmed Hashim, "Shrine Bombing as War's Turning Point Debated," *Washington Post*, March 13, 2007.

20. Jean Hatzfeld, *Machete Season: The Killers in Rwanda Speak* (New York: Farrar, Straus and Giroux, 2005), 76.

21. Mahmood Mamdani, *When Victims Become Killers: Colonialism, Nativism, and the Genocide in Rwanda* (Princeton, NJ: Princeton University Press, 2001), 102. For more on the Hamite Hypothesis, see ch. 3. For more on Sunni Arab perceptions of "Iranians" in Bahrain, see Yitzhak Nakash, *Reaching for Power: The Shi'a in the Modern Arab World* (Princeton, NJ: Princeton University Press, 2006), 19–21.

22. Mamdani, *When Victims Become Killers*, 14.

23. Noel Malcolm, *Kosovo: A Short History* (New York: New York University Press, 1998)

24. Chaim Kaufman, "Possible and Impossible Solutions to Ethnic Civil Wars," *International Security* 20, no. 4 (Spring 1996): 146.

25. See "Ethnic Cleansing in a Baghdad Neighborhood?" *Time*, October 25, 2006. At times, however, the rumor that "lists" are circulating has been used to spread panic and inflame tensions. See Steven L. Burg and Paul S. Shoup, *The War in Bosnia-Herzegovina: Ethnic Conflict and International Intervention* (Armonk, NY: M. E. Sharpe, 1999).

26. Lisa Anderson, "Antiquated Before They Can Ossify: States That Fail Before They Form," *Journal of International Affairs* 58, no. 1 (Fall 2004)

27. Charles Tilly, "Reflections on the History of European State-

Making," in ed. Charles Tilly, The Formation of National States in Western Europe (Princeton: Princeton University Press, 1975), 44.

Additional Readings

Pre-Islamic Civilization

Bauer, Susan Wise. *History of the Ancient World: From the Earliest Acounts to the Fall of Rome*. New York: Norton, 2007.

Bottéro, Jean. *Mesopotamia: Writing, Reasoning, and the Gods*. Translated by Zainab Bahrani and Marc Van De Mieroop. Chicago: University of Chicago Press, 1992.

Frantz, Alison. "From Paganism to Christianity in the Temples of Athens." *Dumbarton Oaks Papers* 19 (1965).

Huart, Clement. *Ancient Persia and Iranian Civilization*. New York: Knopf, 1927.

Kramer, Samuel Noah. *History Begins at Sumer: Thirty-Nine Firsts in Man's Recorded History*. Philadelphia: University of Pennsylvania Press, 1956.

Lewis, Bernard. *The Middle East: 2,000 Years of History from the Rise of Christianity to the Present Day*. London: Weidenfeld & Nicholson, 1995.

Roux, George. *Ancient Iraq*. Harmondsworth, UK: Penguin, 1966.

Salzman, Michele Renee. "The Evidence for the Conversion of the Roman Empire to Christianity in Book 16 of the 'Theodosian Code.'"

Historia: Zeitschrift für Alte Geschichte 42, no. 3 (1993): 362-378.

Treadgold, Warren. *A Concise History of Byzantium.* Houndmills, Basingstoke, Hampshire: Palgrave, 2001.

Whittow, Mark. *The Making of Orthodox Byzantium, 600–1025.* Berkeley: University of California Press, 1996.

Williams, Stephen, and Gerard Friell. *The Rome That Did Not Fall: The Survival of the East in the Fifth Century.* London: Routledge, 1999.

Early Islamic Politics

Aslan, Reza. *No God but God: The Origins, Evolution, and Future of Islam.* New York: Random House, 2005.

Berkey, Jonathan. *The Formation of Islam: Religion and Society in the Near East, 600–1800.* Cambridge, UK: Cambridge University Press, 2002.

Bosworth, Clifford Edmund. T*he Islamic Dynasties: A Chronological and Genealogical Handbook.* Edinburgh: Edinburgh University Press, 1967.

Cooperson, Michael. *Al-Ma'mun.* Oxford: One World, 2005.

Crone, Patricia. *Slaves on Horses: The Evolution of the Islamic Polity.* Cambridge, UK: Cambridge University Press, 1980.

———. *God's Rule—Government and Islam: Six Centuries of Medieval Islamic Political Thought.* New York: Columbia University Press, 2004.

Dabashi, Hamid. *Authority in Islam: From the Rise of Muhammad to the Establishment of the Umayyads.* New Brunswick, NJ: Transaction Publishers, 1989.

Halm, Heinz. *Shi'ism.* 2nd ed. New York: Columbia University Press, 2004.

Hazleton, Lesley. *After the Prophet: The Epic Story of the Shia-Sunni Split in Islam*. New York: Doubleday, 2009.

Hawting, G. R. *The First Dynasty of Islam: The Umayyad Caliphate AD 661–750*. 2nd ed. London: Routledge, 2000.

Hinds, Martin. "The Murder of the Caliph 'Uthman." *International Journal of Middle East Studies* 3, no. 4 (October 1972): 450-469.

Hurvitz, Nimrod. "From Scholarly Circles to Mass Movements: The Formation of Legal Communities in Islamic Societies." *The American Historical Review*, 108, no. 4 (2003): 985-1008.

Kennedy, Hugh. *Early Abbasid Caliphate: A Political History*. London: Croom Helm, 1981.

———. *The Great Arab Conquests: How the Spread of Islam Changed the World We Live In*. New York: Da Capo Press, 2007.

Lapidus, Ira M. "The Separation of State and Religion in the Development of Early Islamic Society." *International Journal of Middle East Studies* 6, no. 4 (1975): 363-385.

Madelung, Wilferd. *The Succession to Muhammad: A Study of the Early Caliphate*. Cambridge, UK: Cambridge University Press, 1997.

Makdisi, George. "The Significance of Sunni Schools of Law in Islamic Religious History." *International Journal of Middle East Studies* 10, no. 1 (1979): 1-8.

Modarressi, Hossein. "Rationalism and Traditionalism in Shi'i Jurisprudence: A Preliminary Survey." *Studia Islamica*, no. 59 (1984): 141-158.

Momen, Moojan. *An Introduction to Shi'i Islam: The History and Doctrines of Twelver Shi'ism*. New Haven: Yale University Press, 1985.

Watt, W. Montgomery. *Early Islam: Collected Articles*. Edinburgh: Edinburgh University Press, 1990.

———. *Muhammad: Prophet and Statesman*. London: Oxford University Press, 1974.

Wiet, Gaston. B*aghdad: Metropolis of the Abbasid Caliphate*. Translated by Seymour Feiler. Norman: University of Oklahoma Press, 1971.

The Middle East in Medieval Times

Amitai-Preiss, Reuven. *Mongols and Mamluks: The Mamluk-Ilkhanid War, 1260–1281*. Cambridge: Cambridge University Press, 1995.

Hallaq, Wael B. "Was the Gate of Ijtihad Closed?" *International Journal of Middle East Studies* 16, no. 1 (1984): 3-41.

Hourani, Albert. "From Jabal Amil to Persia." *Bulletin of the School of Oriental and African Studies* 49, no. 1 (1986): 133-140.

Hunsberger, Alice. *Nasir Khusraw, the Ruby of Badakhshan: A Portrait of the Persian Poet, Traveller, and Philosopher*. London: I. B. Tauris, 2003.

Kortepeter, Carl Max. *Ottoman Imperialism during the Reformation: Europe and the Caucasus*. New York: New York University Press, 1972.

Lewis, Bernard. *The Assassins: A Radical Sect in Islam*. New York: Basic Books, 1968.

Madelung, Wilferd. "The Spread of Maturidism and the Turks." In *Actas, IV Congresso de Estudos Arabes e Islámicos*, Coimbra-Lisboa 1 a 8 de septembro de 1968. Leiden: E. J. Brill, 1971.

Mastnak, Tomaz. "Europe and the Muslims: The Permanent Crusade?" In *The New Crusades: Constructing the Muslim Enemy*, edited by Emran Qureshi and Michael A. Sells. New York: Columbia University Press, 2003.

Morgan, David. *Medieval Persia 1040–1797*. London: Longman, 1988.

Nakash, Yitzhak. "An Attempt to Trace the Origin of the Rituals of Ashura." *Die Welt des Islams* 33, no. 2 (1993): 161-181.

Newman, Andrew J. *Safavid Iran: Rebirth of a Persian Empire*. London: I. B. Tauris, 2006.

Noelles-Karimi, Christine. "Khurasan and Its Limits: Changing Concepts of Territory from Pre-Modern to Modern Times." In *Iran und iranisch geprägte Kulturen*, edited by Markus Ritter, Ralph Kauz, and Birgitt Hoffmann. Wiesbaden: Reichert, 2008.

Rapoport, David C. "Fear and Trembling: Terrorism in Three Religious Traditions." *American Political Science Review* 78, no. 3 (1984): 658-677.

Stanfield Johnson, Rosemary. "Sunni Survival in Safavid Iran: Anti-Sunni Activities during the Reign of Tahmasp I." *Iranian Studies*, 27, no. 1 (1994): 123-133.

Takim, Liyakat A. "From Bid'a to Sunna: The Wilaya of 'Ali in the Shi'i Adhan." *Journal of the American Oriental Society* 120, no. 2 (2000): 166-177.

Walker, Paul E. *Exploring an Islamic Empire: Fatimid History and Its Sources*. London: I. B. Tauris, 2002.

———. "The Ismaili da'wa in the Reign of the Fatimid Caliph al-Hakim," in *Fatimid History and Ismaili Doctrine*. Aldershot, Hampshire: Ashgate/Variorum, 2008.

Yukako, Goto. "The Safavid Court and Its Ceremonies during the Reign of Muhammad Khudabande." In *Iran und iranisch geprägte Kulturen*, edited by Markus Ritter, Ralph Kauz, and Birgitt Hoffmann. Wiesbaden: Reichert, 2008.

Modern Iraq

Allawi, Ali A. *The Occupation of Iraq: Winning the War, Losing the Peace*. New Haven, CT: Yale University Press, 2007.

Balaghi, Shiva. *Saddam Hussein: A Biography.* Westport, CT: Green-wood Press, 2006.

Bengio, Ofra. *Saddam's Word: Political Discourse in Iraq.* New York: Oxford University Press, 1998.

Chandrasekaran, Rajiv. *Imperial Life in the Emerald City: Inside Iraq's Green Zone.* New York: Aflred A. Knopf, 2006.

Chubin, Shahram, and Charles Tripp. *Iran and Iraq at War.* Boulder, CO: Westview Press, 1988.

Cockburn, Patrick. *Muqtada: Muqtada al-Sadr, the Shia Revival, and the Struggle for Iraq.* New York: Scribner, 2008.

Farouk-Sluglett, Marion, and Peter Sluglett. *Iraq Since 1958: From Revolution to Dictatorship.* Rev. ed. London: I. B. Tauris, 2001.

Galbraith, Peter W. *The End of Iraq: How American Incompetence Created a War Without End.* New York: Simon & Shuster, 2006.

Klein, Naomi. *The Shock Doctrine: The Rise of Disaster Capitalism.* New York: Henry Holt, 2007.

Mallat, Chibli. *The Renewal of Islamic Law: Muhammad Baqer as-Sadr, Najaf, and the Shi'i International.* Cambridge: Cambridge Uni-ver-sity Press, 1993.

Marr, Phebe. *The Modern History of Iraq.* 2nd ed. Boulder, CO: Westview Press, 2004.

Nakash, Yitzhak. *Reaching for Power: The Shi'a in the Modern Arab World.* Princeton, NJ: Princeton University Press, 2006.

———. *The Shi'is of Iraq.* 2nd ed. Princeton, NJ: Princeton University Press, 2003.

Nasr, Seyyed Vali Reza. *The Shia Revival: How Conflicts within Islam Will Shape the Future.* New York: Norton, 2006.

Ricks, Thomas E. *Fiasco: The American Military Adventure in Iraq.* New York: Penguin Press, 2007.

———. *The Gamble: General David Petraeus and the American Military*

Adventure in Iraq, 2006-2008. New York: Penguin Press, 2009.

Roston, Aram. *The Man Who Pushed America to War: The Extraordinary Life, Adventures, and Obsessions of Ahmed Chalabi*. New York: Nation Books, 2008.

Sluglett, Peter. *Britain in Iraq: Contriving King and Country, 1914–1932*. London: I. B. Tauris, 2007.

Sluglett, Peter, and Marion Farouk-Sluglett. "Some Reflections on the Sunni/Shiʻi Question in Iraq." *Bulletin* (British Society for Middle East Studies) 5, no. 2 (1978): 79-87.

Ethnic and Sectarian Conflict

Anderson, Lisa. "Antiquated Before They Can Ossify: States That Fail Before They Form." *Journal of International Affairs* 58, no. 1 (2004)

Betts, Richard K. "The Delusion of Impartial Intervention." *Foreign Affairs* 73, no. 6 (November–December 1994): 20-32.

Burg, Steven L., and Paul S. Shoup. *The War in Bosnia-Herzegovina: Ethnic Conflict and International Intervention*. Armonk, NY: M. E. Sharpe, 1999.

Firro, Kais M. *Inventing Lebanon: Nationalism and the State under the Mandate*. London: I. B. Tauris, 2003,

Friedman, Thomas L. *From Beirut to Jerusalem*. New York: Anchor Books, 1995,

Byman, Daniel L. "Divided They Stand: Lessons about Partitioning from Iraq and Lebanon," *Security Studies*, 7, no. 1 (1997)

Hatzfeld, Jean. *Machete Season: The Killers in Rwanda Speak*. New York: Farrar, Straus and Giroux, 2005.

Huntington, Samuel P. *Political Order in Changing Societies*. New Haven, CT: Yale Univeristy Press, 1968. 2007.

Jenkins, J. Craig, and Esther E. Gottlieb, eds. *Identity Conflicts: Can Violence Be Regulated?* New Brunswick, NJ: Transaction Publishers, 2007.

Kaufman, Chaim. "Possible and Impossible Solutions to Ethnic Civil Wars." *International Security* 20, no. 4 (1996): 136-175.

———. "When All Else Fails: Ethnic Population Transfers and Partitions in the Twentieth Century," *International Security*, 23, no. 2 (1998): 120-156.

———. "A Security Dilemma: Ethnic Partitioning in Iraq," *Ethnic Conflict*, 28, no. 4 (2007)

Malcolm, Noel. *Kosovo: A Short History.* New York: New York University Press, 1998.

Mamdani, Mahmood. *When Victims Become Killers: Colonialism, Nativism, and the Genocide in Rwanda.* Princeton, NJ: Princeton University Press, 2001.

Posen, Barry R. "The Security Dilemma and Ethnic Conflict." *Survival* 35, no. 1 (1993): 27-47.

Power, Samantha. *A Problem from Hell: America and the Age of Genocide.* New York: Basic Books, 2002.

Schlee, Günther, ed. *Imagined Differences: Hatred and the Construction of Identity.* Münster, Germany: Lit Verlag, 2002.

Snyder, Jack. *From Voting to Violence: Democratization and Nationalist Conflict.* New York: Norton, 2000.

Tilly, Charles, ed. *The Formation of National States in Western Europe.* Princeton, NJ: Princeton University Press, 1975.

Wedgwood, C. V. *The Thirty Years War.* London: Penguin Books, 1957.

Index*

* For clarity, Imams are numbered according to Twelver Shia tradition. Also note that the
definite article al- is omitted from names.

About the Author

NATHAN GONZALEZ is a Fellow with the Truman National Security Project and author of *Engaging Iran: The Rise of a Middle East Powerhouse and America's Strategic Choice* (2007). In 2002, he received the Dean's Prize for Undergraduate Research from the University of California-Los Angeles for his research on Iraq, through which he predicted that U.S. invasion would bring about massive sectarian violence and a stronger Iran. He holds a Master of International Affairs from Columbia University and is currently a doctoral student in political science at UCLA.

For more information visit: www.NathanGonzalez.com